The Path of the Warrior

An Ethical Guide to Personal and Professional Development in the Field of Criminal Justice

By Larry F. Jetmore, Ph.D.

Looseleaf Law Publications, Inc.

43-08 162nd Street
Flushing, NY 11358
(718) 359-5559 also FAX (718) 539-0941
www.LooseleafLaw.com   llawpub@erols.com

ACKNOWLEDGMENTS

This book would not have been possible without the expert guidance of my editor, Linnea Fredrickson. So as one warrior to another I tip my hat and lift a cup of cheer knowing this work would not have been readable without her.

This book is dedicated to my five grandchildren, Sean Jr., Joshua, Brianna, Brandon, and Tyler, all warriors in the making.

Larry F. Jetmore, Ph.D.

ISBN 1-889031-05-4

Also by Larry F. Jetmore:

Cliffs Police Management Examinations Preparation Guide
Cliffs Police Officer Examination Preparation Guide
Cliffs Police Sergeant Examination Preparation Guide

For information regarding these titles, contact:

Cliffs Notes, Inc.
P.O. Box 80728
Lincoln, NE 68501
800-228-4078

Cover: Badges provided by Smith & Warren Co.
127 Oakley Ave., White Plains, NY 10601

Table of Contents

About the Author

Larry F. Jetmore, Ph.D., is a twenty-one year veteran and former captain and commander of the Hartford, Connecticut, Police Department Investigative Services Bureau. He has held a variety of patrol investigative, and training commands throughout his career including command of the vice and narcotics division and the special weapons assault team. Dr. Jetmore received a doctorate in organizational development and criminology from the Union Institute in Cincinnati, Ohio; a master's degree in education and a bachelor's degree in business from Eastern Connecticut State University; and an associate degree in criminal justice from Manchester Community College. He has written three textbooks in the field of criminal justice and teaches courses at several colleges in New England while maintaining a national consulting practice for police and private security agencies.

Preface

This book is written for police officers and students of law enforcement who are searching for practical ways to resolve the complicated ethical dilemmas faced by those who wear a badge and carry a gun. It also has utility for others in the care-giving professions who are questioning the significance of the work they do and who want to make positive changes in their personal and professional lives. Many professionals are experiencing various stages of disillusionment resulting from the value conflicts, cynicism, and social isolation that are often byproducts of working in occupations with a great deal of trauma.

People who have chosen policing as a way of life are especially vulnerable to a slow draining of enthusiasm and positive energy. In giving so much of themselves to others, over time it becomes increasingly difficult to rekindle the fire that first drew them to policing. What I try to do in this book is offer a different way of thinking and living—provide intervention techniques—that many have found helpful in guarding their inner spirits while going where others fear to tread.

Answering the question, How does today's police officer determine the 'right' thing to do? is the primary focus of this work. Through personal accounts, interviews, a study of ancient skills, and a look at the wisdom offered by various sages, this book brings together some of the best thinking on this question. We will explore different paths to taking positive control of our lives and stimulating personal and professional growth.

🌓 Introduction

When I finally decided to "pull the pin" and retire after twenty-one years with the Hartford, Connecticut, police department, I thought the transition to civilian life would be easy. I was relatively young, my pension was more than what most people earn working full time, and I looked forward to working on my doctorate and teaching criminal justice courses. I also envisioned retirement as an opportunity to write police textbooks, do a little consulting, and enjoy my five grandchildren. All of this came to pass. There is life after policing, and it's as rich and wonderful as you could imagine. The check comes every month, and I purposefully do not have it electronically deposited in my bank account because I want to open the envelope, see the numbers, and feel the paper in my hands.

The only catch I've found is that since policing is a *way of life,* as opposed to a job or even a career, I have never really gotten being a cop out of my blood. It's permanent. Not even remembering the midnight shift, department politics, or working holidays alters the fact that I no longer have the power to significantly affect the lives of others—to do good—as I once did. I miss policing, and my retirement check and the time to enjoy life hasn't seemed to change that. Also, it wasn't until I retired and gained the capacity to look into the police world from outside that I fully realized how remarkable the police officers I served with are.

As I taught criminal justice courses at various Connecticut colleges and universities and my police textbooks got out in the national market, my contacts with officers from outside of New England increased dramatically. I began receiving calls to lecture at criminal justice and human resource training seminars and workshops around the country. Over the past several years, I've spoken at length with hundreds of police officers, and as a result have become more and more concerned that the rich heritage and most cherished traditions of policing are not being passed along from cop to cop as they once were. Unfortunately, many of the officers I've spoken with view policing as just a job rather than a unique way of life. For a variety of reasons, the type of "mentoring" I grew accustomed to receiving, and in turn giving, no longer seems to be occurring. Our officers are left like corks bobbing on the water without role models to guide them and instill the ideals and moral principles so important in police work. Of greater consequence is the fact that many of our young officers don't even realize something important is missing. What's missing is a central core of values to help them choose between alternative courses of action when all of them may appear to be the "right" thing to do.

So, I have written this book for and about police officers—men and women who have chosen a *way of life* characterized by serving and helping others. Its purpose is to provide police officers and students of law enforcement with a framework leading to ethical behavior, personal development, growth, and professional success. I use the symbolic term *warrior* in this book because police officers engage in a continuous struggle of the inner spirit to produce and sustain the positive energy necessary to share their light with others.

The struggle to "serve and protect" is becoming increasingly difficult because we are living at a time of social upheaval where belief systems and values are clashing. Our society has devalued many of the virtues it exalted not so long ago. Integrity, self-discipline, courage, honor, devotion to duty, and ethical behavior, to name just a few of them, have become confusing concepts in an era of self-indulgence and an "I" mentality. Accepting individual responsibility for our own behavior and, ultimately, our own happiness has become a blurry concept. Many individuals seem to sway with the will of the majority rather than navigate from deep personal conviction and rational thought.

We are also living in a time of "the claw and the fang," where the care-giving aspects of policing are practiced in an environment of hopelessness, despair, and corruption. Those who have dedicated their lives to having a positive influence on other people are continually exposed to overwhelming traumatic experiences akin to military combat: drive-by shootings, murders, the affects of drugs, suicides, widespread homelessness, exposure to AIDS, domestic violence, poverty, child abuse, and the list goes on and on. One only needs to see an inner city emergency room or local precinct house for a few hours to experience the horror in which our officers work every day. It's little wonder that many of our police officers have become disillusioned, burned out, and engaged in a variety of self-destructive behaviors that devalue themselves and their professions.

Other officers are just plain unhappy. They have lost the joy that the gift of service to others, to community, and to country once brought them. At training programs, seminars, and on retreats, they describe to me a feeling of isolation and emptiness—an "inner hunger." They have lost their *shadows,* the certainty that their lives have significance and that being in law enforcement is meaningful.

It doesn't have to be this way! Police officers *can* live lives of service to others while living lives of joy, fulfillment, and happiness. It is possible if you open your heart and mind and begin walking the path of a *warrior.* But beware! The techniques offered in this book are not for the fainthearted. There are no quick fixes and effortless solutions. The very fact that you're reading this book means you have answered the call to adventure, are seeking new frontiers, and want to open the gate leading to the path. That's good. You have taken a positive step in recognizing that police officers march to the beat of a different drummer, and you are moving toward self-affirming thoughts and behavior. Inner knowing is a lifelong journey with many traps and dragons along the path to the way. My hope is that this book will provide today's *warriors* with some useful techniques in the form of shields and amulets so their light will burn brightly and they can find their shadow again. What is offered in this text does not claim to be the *only* way; rather it is intended to be a framework to assist you on your journey to develop your full potential.

Larry F. Jetmore, Ph. D.

viii

CHAPTER 1

Ethics and the Police

The human being needs a framework of values, a philosophy of life,
a religion or religion-surrogate to live by and understand by,
in about the same sense that he needs sunlight, calcium, or love.

Abraham Maslow

The ethical decisions confronting the police in a democracy are so extraordinary that there is no other occupation in which its members are and should be held to such a high standard of professional and personal conduct. Translating the ideals of police ethics into everyday police behavior is the task of every person who wears a badge and carries a gun. Because police work consists almost entirely of service to people and is concerned primarily with human behavior, the success or failure of a police organization depends heavily on the actions of its individual members.

Several factors unique to law enforcement contribute to public criticism about the conduct of police officers:

- Police service is one of the few "businesses" in which a large part of the clientele does not appreciate or want the service.

- Police officers are usually easily recognizable because of the uniforms they wear and their conspicuously marked vehicles. This makes their actions or inactions more noticeable than those of people in other occupations.

- Enforcement of the law often creates resentment of the police, especially if officers' actions are perceived to be selective, arbitrary, or aimed at a particular group of people.

- Police officers are exposed to temptations, situations, and human behaviors not found in other forms of work.

- Police officers often work without supervision, are vested with extraordinary power to control the conduct and behavior of the people they serve, and frequently make decisions about the delivery of police services at their own discretion.

- Police officers are involved in emotionally charged and dangerous situations, such as arrests, detainment, and the use of force, which may compromise the reason and judgment of both officers and citizens (Wilson 1977).

The public expects police officers to exhibit a higher level of personal and professional conduct than people in other occupations. Due to the high visibility of police officers and the enormous powers granted to them by society, members of the community are apt to be more critical of police misconduct than bad behavior in other occupations. Although the standards outlined in the "Canons of Police Ethics" will be discussed in chapter 3, to do so requires laying the groundwork relevant to the different ethical systems having the most influence on policing, so we can understand how they relate to the subject of police ethics.

☯ WHAT ARE ETHICS?

The term *ethics* is derived from the Greek word *ethos,* meaning "customary behavior." We study ethics to identify the norms or standards that should guide people in controlling their conduct. Ethics is also concerned with attempting to define what is "good" for individuals and for society. Typical definitions include such phrases as "the study of human conduct to determine what actions are good and what kinds are bad," "a set of moral principles or values," and "the study of human conduct according to standards of good and evil discoverable by reason." The word *morals* is often used interchangeably with *ethics* and is derived from the Latin *mos* or *moris,* meaning "custom, habit, or way of life."

From before the time of Christ on through the centuries to the present, the teaching of ethics and morals has centered on what it is "good" or "bad" and what a person "ought" or "ought not" do. The names you will come across in a study of ethics will include the ancient Greeks, such as Socrates, Plato, and Aristotle; Jesus Christ; St. Augustine of Hippo and St. Thomas Aquinas; and the early moderns (late sixteenth through the nineteenth century) such as Thomas Hobbes, Jeremy Bentham, Immanuel Kant, Francis Bacon, and John Stuart Mill. Each of these moral philosophers had a different opinion of what constituted "good" or "bad" conduct.

The difficulty in deciding what is "right" and "wrong" has led philosophers to divide into two camps. One side says there are no moral standards that apply to everyone. People must decide what is right depending on the situation. The other side says there are moral standards that apply to everyone, and people have an obligation to do what is known to be right. The reason this is important to police officers is that deciding what is right or wrong is a large part of what police officers do. Statute books are full of laws, but it is the police officer who decides under what circumstances to enforce them.

The major questions often posed to students in ethics and philosophy courses are:

1. What is "good"? According to what standard? How do we define it?

2. How do we determine what is the "right" thing to do? In regard to what?

3. Who determines whether another person "ought" to behave in a certain manner? The individual? the community? the society?

4. What specific behavior(s) determines whether the action or inaction of a person is "good" or "bad"? the person's motive or intent? the end result?

5. Are "right" and "wrong" relative terms depending on a person's point of view?

Many claim there is little to be gained from the study of ethics. They might say that because we all intuitively know through the ordinary experiences of life the difference between such terms as "right" and "wrong" and "good" and "bad" that defining those terms by way of different schools of esoteric academic thought is of little use in practical, everyday life. Some skeptics argue that ethics are little more than the vigorous assertion of the will of a group of people living together in a community, and that since the truth can never be absolutely known, ideas of right and wrong are matters of personal preference or cultural choice. They would say that entire cultures have performed terrible acts on other people and have justified their actions on the basis of some greater "good."

The skeptics miss the point that the study of ethics provides a way to make choices when there is uncertainty about what is the right thing to do. Ethics begin when we ask ourselves, "How should I live my life?" Rather than restricting people to specific moral options and binding obligations, ethics serve as a lens through which to view choices during the course of one's life. Knowledge of ethics allows a process by which a rational human being existing in the world of nature can strive toward goodness by focusing on the development of character.

The idea of the "will of a group of people" having a strong influence on the conduct of its members is especially relevant to ethics in policing because police forces are primarily male-dominated, closed, isolated semi-military societies with rites of passage not found in other vocations. Police officers routinely deal with highly emotional, often bizarre situations outside the range of the average person's experience. The police work in a world of people preying on one another, a world where a crack addict's "fried" brain lets him shoot a woman just to get the money from her purse to buy a few more vials of drugs, a world of guns, stabbings, and drive-by shootings. Contacts between officers and citizens are often adversary in nature, full of tension and hostility. However well police officers do their jobs, they are criticized by the people they serve and those they take action against. These and other factors that will be discussed later cause the police to see themselves as members of a group aligned against common enemies.

Terms such as "the thin blue line," the police "code of silence," the "blue curtain" and "the only color we know is blue" reflect the secretive and tribal aspects that make policing so different from other occupations. Police officers are heavily dependent on one another in emergency situations where their lives are in danger, such as in a fight or shoot-out. The discretionary nature of police decision making and the disparity between official policy and the actual performing of the job on the street result in a rationalizing of conduct as being in the best interest of the public. All of these factors contribute to a closed work environment, making it unlikely tha. one officer will "rat" on another officer's improper conduct. To do so would ostracize the "ratting" officer from the group and subject him or her to harassment and tremendous pressure from fellow police officers, making it difficult to continue working as an officer.

The facts mentioned above illustrate the influence a police officer's peers have on an officer's ethical decision making. It seems easier to avoid ostracism and criticism and just go along with the group. However, when we choose to do what we know is wrong, it will always result in paying the piper later, as you will see as you read on in this book.

☯ Situational Ethics

The danger in *not* having a basic understanding of the various ethical systems is overlooking the universality of the core values contained within each that *can* be applied to everyday living. With no way to determine what is right or wrong, the tendency is to drift toward a kind of "situational ethics" as defined by American Protestant theologian Joseph Fletcher. In situational ethics, "anything and everything is right or wrong according to the situation" and "there are no such things as values, everything has a price, and only the ends justify the means" (Fletcher 1966). In other words, there are no objective standards that apply to everyone, and people must decide what is good for others as well as themselves based on the situation.

Many of today's law enforcement officers seem to have drifted toward this "situational ethics" viewpoint. When we hear police officers make statements such as, "If it's legal, it's ethical," we know they are speaking from a situational ethics rationalization of behavior. Rationalization is a form of self-alibi to avoid a loss of self-esteem and prevent feelings of guilt. However, "If it's legal, it's ethical" is the same rationale used by the Nazis at the Nuremberg trials to defend their actions in the concentration camps during World War II.

From that short phrase, it is only a small step to "the ends justify the means." In policing, catching the bad guy—a good intent—is used as a justification for illegal wiretapping, planting evidence, swearing to false information in affidavits supporting arrest and search warrants, using verbal and physical abuse, and other misuses of police authority.

☯ The Dirty Harry Syndrome

Are there any circumstances in which a police officer should violate the law in order to protect the public? For example, what if a police officer is absolutely certain a suspect knows where a kidnapped child is being held? The officer is certain because the suspect admitted he had taken the child and knows details about the case that only someone directly involved in the kidnapping could know. Although the suspect admits to the kidnapping, he will not tell the officer where the child is. Is it then permissible for the officer to beat the man—torture him—until he tells the officer where the child is located? If it were your child who had been kidnapped rather than a stranger's, would you condone the officer's actions if he beat the suspect? What if the child is diabetic, needs insulin, and if not quickly found will die? Under these circumstances, would it be permissible for the officer to beat the suspect so the child's life could be saved?

This type of scenario has been referred to as a "Dirty Harry problem," after the popular Clint Eastwood character who often violated the law "to protect the public" (Klockard 1989). There are good reasons why there are *no* circumstances in which torturing a suspect by a police officer is permissible. *Quis custodiet ipsos custodes?* Who guards the guardians? The Fifth Amendment to our Constitution provides that we cannot be forced to give evidence that could help convict us. Police officers are direct representatives of the government. The American system of criminal justice rests on a philosophy that recognizes justice is based on a respect for the dignity of the individual. A person is innocent until proven guilty in a court of law, and the government must play by the "rules of the game" in proving its case against the defendant. In a free and democratic society, if the police violate the law to obtain evidence that a person has committed a crime, then in a sense the government is supporting criminal activity. The scriptural refrain that "one may not do evil so that good may result from it" is appropriate here.

Regardless of the motive or intent, there is *never* justification for police officers to break the law or use unethical methods to enforce it. Do you see why it is so important to have a thorough grounding in ethics to prepare for a career in law enforcement? Our system of policing is based on the belief that the power of police officers to fulfill their functions and duties is dependent on the public approval of their existence, actions, and behavior, and on their ability to secure and maintain public respect (Reith 1948).

Even in the case of the kidnapped diabetic child who may die from insulin shock if not quickly located, there are good reasons why we don't allow a police officer to torture a suspect to obtain information. What are they? History has shown us time and time again that human beings are fallible, and even when defendants' constitutional rights have been strictly adhered to, they have sometimes confessed to the police crimes that they did not commit, and they have been sentenced to prison.

In our example, the suspect told the officer he kidnapped the child, and according to the officer "knows details about the case that only someone directly involved in the kidnapping could know." Those of you who think it is OK to torture the suspect are relying on the police officer to be correct in his or her assessment. Suppose the officer is wrong? What if a combination of factors are at work here, such as the suspect being mentally ill or deficient and the officer being a person who enjoys torturing people. What if the officer thinks the suspect has information only the kidnapper could have, but is wrong? Does our society want to give that much power—the authority to beat and torture people—to the police, or any other agency of the government? Of course not. It is rare that something like this occurs in modern law enforcement, and there are alternative methods of interrogating suspects that have a very high success rate and are within the parameters of legal and ethical behavior. Learning how to properly obtain information from people takes years of practice and study. We admire Sherlock Holmes and the popular television detective Columbo because both used their minds to gather facts leading to the solution of crimes. We expect our police officers to follow their example.

We will be discussing why the application of ethics is especially important in law enforcement throughout this book, but to familiarize you with the reasoning behind some of the major schools of ethical thought, a brief summary of each is found in the chart below.

MAJOR ETHICAL SCHOOLS OF THOUGHT

End-results Ethics	Duty-based Ethics	Hebrew/Christian Ethics
Utilitarianism	Categorical Imperative	The Perfect Good
Jeremy Bentham (1748-1832) John Stuart Mill (1806-1873)	Immanuel Kant (1712-1804)	St. Thomas Aquinas (1225-1274)
The "rightness" of an action is to be found in the greatest good for the greatest number of people.	Act so that your individual action might become a general rule for all.	God is the objective end. One's conscience decides what is right or wrong.
Relies on evaluating the end results or consequences of an action. You know what is right only by determining what eventually occurs.	The moral rightness of an action is determined by laws and standards.	The Golden Rule: "Do unto others as you would have others do unto you."

🌓 Social Contract Theory

The reason the police as an institution and its individual members are held to such high ethical standards has a long history steeped in the traditions of Judeo-Christian religious morality and philosophy. America strongly reflects a Judeo-Christian heritage in the melting pot that makes up our nation. Our government, its oldest documents (the Declaration of Independence and the U.S. Constitution), its laws, and our heritage strongly reflect a belief in God who makes each person in his own image.

Foremost among these traditions is that American democratic society and the laws that govern the conduct of its people are firmly grounded in what has come to be known as "social contract theory." The founder of social contract theory, Jean Jacques Rousseau

(1712–1778), one of the great political philosophers, challenged kingly authority and sought the key to balancing a person's individual freedom against the collective security offered by organized governmental authority.

Rousseau concluded that this balance could be accomplished only if "each member of society gives up a certain amount of freedom through the support and protection of the community" (Rousseau [1762] 1947). Essentially, this is the basic rationale underlying the United States Constitution and its Bill of Rights. In other words, in a broad sense the individual members of society as a whole determine the standard for what is moral or immoral, what is lawful or unlawful, and what is "good" or "bad." Societies establish rules or standards defining basic principles of what is "good" and this furthers the welfare of the entire group. These standards set by society are codified into civil and criminal laws, which the majority of the people theoretically consent to and are binding on each of its individual members. Laws are necessary to control conduct, not because people agree, but because they disagree.

An outgrowth of social contract theory is what Dr. William Hitt, an author of several books on leadership and ethics, calls "social contract ethics." Social contract ethics states that "the moral rightness of an action is determined by the customs and norms of a particular community" (Hitt 1990). The basic police mandates of serving and protecting the public and the essence of the various police powers—to arrest, detain, use force, and search people, for example—have their foundation firmly rooted in social contract ethics. The balancing of a person's right to individual freedom against the collective security offered by government is the difficult task law enforcement officers face each day. The actions or inactions of individual police officers are often judged by the general public—the community—in terms of social contract ethics.

Notice it's the general public and *not* the organization of the police department or the courts that do the judging. They use different ethical systems. Police organizations and the court system use a combination of what Dr. Hitt calls "end-result ethics" and "rule ethics" to determine whether a person's behavior—mode of conduct—has been determined by society to be morally correct.

End-result ethics were defined by John Stuart Mill. Most of the noted English philosophers in the eighteenth and nineteenth century wrote on ethics, and Mill became famous for his theory that "the moral rightness of an action is determined by its consequences." Mill thought that when making ethical decisions the rule should be to "do the greatest good for the greatest number."

Rule ethics were defined by another famous eighteenth-century philosopher named Immanuel Kant to mean "The moral rightness of an action is determined by laws and standards" (Kant 1963). Rule ethics embody the concept that "we are a nation of laws, not of men" and that all conduct in violation of the law must be punished. In direct contrast is the premise that in a free society, limits are placed on the authority and the power of the law to control the behavior of the people. Compromising between arbitrary law, which is the result of rule ethics, and individual conduct resulting from personal morality is the task of all human beings living in a communal society. The idea that society uses the police as initial determiners of whether conduct is outside the norms it has established is what makes police discretionary decision making so difficult and ethical conduct so essential.

To regulate police conduct and behavior, limit the discretionary power of police officers, and provide for the efficient and effective delivery of police services, police departments create policies and procedures and specific rules and regulations for its members to abide by. However, no law, rule, or regulation can be written with such specificity as to cover every type of situation individual officers encounter. The great ambiguity between the vagueness of laws and police policy and procedure allows officers to exercise broad discretionary judgment in the decision-making process. It's in this broad area of police discretion that the individual ethics of police officers play a key role. It is only through individual ethics—let's define it as the realization that the moral rightness of an action is determined by one's conscience, not by social contract ethics or rule ethics—that officers can make decisions taking into account what is practical, possible, and ethical. As Dr. Gerald F. Kreyche, professor emeritus of philosophy at Depaul University, wrote, "moral authority is not bestowed, but is based on right conduct and the depth of one's character and personal commitment" (Kreyche, 1993). So, it is in the balancing of these differing ethical systems that the individual police officer must ultimately make choices between alternative courses of action. If all this entailed was simply choosing between good and evil, with no gray area in between, the ethical dilemmas faced by law enforcement officers would be relatively easy. However, the real difficulty for the police officer is in making choices between two or more alternative courses of action, each of which may appear to be the "right" thing to do. Consider that

- it may be *right* for a police officer to arrest a person who has committed a crime and *right* not to.

- it may be *right* for a police officer to shoot a person pointing a gun at him, her, or another person and *right* not to.

- it may be *right* for a police officer to arrest one person addicted to drugs and *right* to take another substance abuser to a hospital.

- it may be *right* for an off-duty police officer to engage in a police strike and *right* not to.

- it may be *right* for a police officer to give a motorist a ticket for speeding and *right* not to.

- it may be *right* for a police officer to truthfully answer questions in court and *right* not to volunteer information if not asked.

- it may be *right* for a police officer to use a great deal of force in making an arrest and *right* not to.

- it may be *right* for a police officer to search a person and *right* not to.

It is in this "right vs. right" arena that the most difficult choices facing a law enforcement officer can be found (Kidder 1996).

This is not to imply that right vs. wrong choices do not involve ethical decisions, but only that they are easier to resolve and do not require the depth of searching one's basic values that right vs. right dilemmas do. To make this perfectly clear, some examples of right vs. wrong decisions follow.

- It is always *wrong* for a police officer to steal and always *right* not to.?

- It is always *wrong* for a police officer to fabricate evidence and always *right* not to.

- It is always *wrong* for a police officer to lie in court and always *right* not to.

- It is always *wrong* for a police officer to mistreat a prisoner and always *right* not to and not to allow others to do so.

- It is always *wrong* for a police officer to accept a bribe or gratuity and always *right* not to.

- It is always *wrong* for a police officer to intentionally use excessive force and always *right* not to.

- It is always *wrong* to use duress, force, or threat to coerce a confession and always *right* not to.

- It is always *wrong* for a police officer to treat people disrespectfully and always *right* for a police officer to treat people respectfully.

- It is always *wrong* for a police officer to show favoritism to one person or group and always *right* not to.

Right vs. wrong choices are easily identified, and there is universal agreement that crimes committed by police officers are wrong. Everyone agrees that police corruption is unethical. Whether it's bribery and extortion, appropriating items at a crime scene and blaming the theft on criminals, or taking items from a store whose door was left open, all are criminal acts. There is little room for discussion here. The difficulty remains in distinguishing the "right" thing to do when several different courses of action have components of "rightness" attached to them.

War Story

An example may help. A police officer on foot patrol surprises three youths sharing a marijuana cigarette in a secluded area of a city park. All three begin running when they spot the officer, but one boy is so overweight that he moves only a few yards before giving up. The other two get away. While speaking with the youth, the officer observes that the boy is so scared he has urinated in his pants. She learns the young man's name is Benjamin Saunders and that he has asthma. She finds an asthma inhaler in the boy's jacket pocket.

Benjamin turned sixteen yesterday, which means he is no longer a juvenile and can be arrested, handcuffed, and booked in the adult system. The officer retrieves the partially smoked marijuana cigarette, and Benjamin begins to cry. He reveals that this is the first time he had been invited by his two friends, both of whom are fifteen, to go anywhere with them. Even though smoke of any kind makes him sick, he agreed to come with the two boys to smoke the marijuana, fearing that if he didn't he would never be asked to go anywhere with them again. He reluctantly gives the officer the names of the other two, who, like himself, live a short distance from the park.

What is the *right* thing for the officer to do? Marijuana is illegal. Benjamin and the other two youths have committed a crime. The officer is on patrol in the park specifically because people have complained about groups of youths using drugs there. Would the officer be *right* if she placed Benjamin in handcuffs, took him to the police station, had him sign a statement admitting his guilt and incriminating the other two youths, and then booked him? Would the officer be *right* to pick up the other two youths and refer them to the juvenile system since they are under the age of sixteen? That's the law. Isn't that the officer's job? What happens to Benjamin and the other boys is not her problem. After all, they made the choice to break the law. Three arrests and the confiscation of even a partially smoked marijuana cigarette will please the officer's supervisors because they can point to the arrests as a proactive response to citizen complaints about youth drug use in the parks.

Would it also be *right* for the officer not to arrest anyone? Would it be *right* for the officer to take into consideration all of the information known about the case, take Benjamin home, and advise his parents about what had happened; to also tell the parents of the other two youths; to turn the marijuana in to the police property room; and to submit a police report detailing those actions?

Would it be *right* after sizing up the situation for the officer to say to Benjamin, "Here's what could happen. I could arrest you and put you in handcuffs. I could take you to the station and then go round up those two buddies of yours and arrest them. Your picture and fingerprints will be taken, and your parents will have to come to the police station to get you out. You'll go to court and may have an arrest record for the rest of your life. However, I'm not going to do any of that. I'm going to give you a break and let you go. This is the one and only break you'll get from me. I'll be keeping an eye out for you. Now take off."

There are many other possible variations to this scenario, and the adding or subtracting of certain details might change what the *right* action is. However, in the case illustrated, all three courses of action have components of *rightness* about them. What do you think is the *right* thing for the officer to do? Virtues such as compassion, mercy, and forgiveness often clash with other virtues, such as justice and prudence. Choices must be made, often weighing one good against another.

One sort of police officer wouldn't see the situation involving Benjamin as being an ethical dilemma at all. "If you can't do the time, don't do the crime." This officer would arrest Benjamin and not give the matter another thought. Another sort of police officer would quickly realize that although a law had been broken, Benjamin is not a "criminal." The *right* thing to do may be to choose the middle ground and take Benjamin home. This sort of officer might spend some time afterward thinking about whether just taking Benjamin home had been the right thing to do. Which of the two officers would you prefer to have working in your community?

In the arena in which policing takes place, there are often times when an officer reasons out the 'right' thing to do, but then fails to translate morality into action. This failure to act results from not wanting to appear "soft" in the eyes of his or her peers. Ethical decision making is often strongly influenced by group pressure. Since the ground rules for judging appropriate and inappropriate behavior are embedded in police culture, part of the reason for the failure is in understanding the unique world of the "claw and the fang" in which policing takes place. I call it "living between worlds."

It's easier to fight for one's principles than to live up to them.

Adlai Stevenson

☯ LIVING BETWEEN WORLDS

So why *are* the police held to a higher standard of professional and personal conduct than are members of any other profession? Why is it that when *one* police officer is publicized for unethical conduct, *all* members of that department are often judged by the public to be unethical? And, importantly for the purpose of this book, what exactly do ethics, character, and values have to do with *your* individual job satisfaction, personal and professional growth, and attainment of a fulfilling life? Understanding the answers to these questions provides a framework on which we can build principles that help eliminate the complexity and confusion surrounding the ethical decisions made by today's law enforcement officers.

To put police ethics into perspective, let's recognize that policing is not a job in the traditional sense, nor even a career. Policing is a "way of life." The difference is important. The police culture has a dramatic effect on the behavior of police officers. As stated before, police officers are very much a tribe, a cloistered semi-military society, still largely male dominated, that has definitive rites of passage and rigid standards of behavior that can't be found in other vocations. Due to the nature of police work, most behavior that is unethical is witnessed by other police officers. When asked by supervisors about the alleged misconduct of another officer, most choose to remain silent or say they didn't see anything. This "code of secrecy" in the police culture helps to insulate unethical and corrupt officers from being separated from police service or prosecuted under the law. The axiom "You're either with us or against us" is a common refrain in policing, reflecting that the police stick together as a group and view everyone else as the enemy. The police culture has been described as having six core beliefs:

1. The police are the only real crime fighters. The public wants the police officer to fight crime; other agencies, both public and private, only play at crime fighting.

2. No one else understands the real nature of police work. Lawyers, academics, politicians, and the general public have little concept of what it means to be a police officer.

3. Loyalty to colleagues counts above everything else. Police officers have to stick together because everyone is out to get the police and make the job more difficult.

4. It is impossible to win the war against crime without bending the rules. Courts have awarded criminal defendants too many civil rights.

5. Members of the public are basically unsupportive and unreasonably demanding. People are quick to criticize the police unless they need the police themselves.

6. Patrol work is the pits. Detective work is glamorous and exciting (Kennedy 1990).

The core belief system of the police culture is important because beliefs directly affect behavior. There is a direct conflict between the six cultural beliefs listed above and the ideals expressed in the police code of ethics, which will be discussed later in the book. Failure to resolve the conflict between the reality of working within the police culture and the idealism of the "Law Enforcement Code of Ethics" often produces a progressive loss of enthusiasm, energy, and purpose, leading to apathy and burnout. It is in the area between the behavior affirmed by the police culture and an officer's desire to fulfill the elusive ideals embodied in the police creed that ethical decision making is most difficult.

The "way of life" outlined in the law enforcement code of ethics requires police officers to model behavior that would be a challenge to most religious orders. Officers are expected to make a lifelong commitment to ethical ideals few are able to sustain over time. Why? Because the right thing to do becomes confusing when your work constantly exposes you to criminals who have no ethics. This, coupled with the fact that the police culture circles the wagons at any hint of criticism about how police officers do their jobs, requires an ethical person to make choices that may be viewed by peers as weakness or professional incompetence. Self-discipline and strong character help a person think through decisions and see the alternatives between ethical and unethical behavior.

War Story

Another example may help here. A police sergeant recently told me of an ethical dilemma, which on the face of it seems simple to resolve unless you understand the inner workings of the police culture. The sergeant was in charge of a crime analysis unit in a large, metropolitan police department. A major part of the unit's function was police report review and the classification of each crime into a particular category according to guidelines established by the Federal Bureau of Investigation (FBI) for compiling its quarterly uniform crime report. For example, members of the unit would read a report of a purse snatching, make a determination based on the FBI guidelines whether the circumstances surrounding the purse snatching constituted a larceny or a robbery, and record the case as one or the other. In addition to reporting these statistics to the FBI, the crime analysis unit produced a quarterly report for the department comparing crimes committed in the current year with crimes from the same period the previous year. The report was distributed to the chief of police and his command staff and also to various civic organizations and members of the community. Because the chief and the rest of the department are judged largely on whether crime has risen or declined, the report is political dynamite.

The sergeant told me that crime in the city for the past quarter was generally down, with the notable exception of burglary. The chief had an upcoming meeting with the city council to review the department's budget for the following year. In a private meeting in the chief's office, the sergeant was informed that it would be "great" if something could be done to show that burglaries had also declined. The sergeant was instructed to review the burglary cases for the past quarter and see if they could be reclassified as criminal trespass or theft, both of which are relatively minor crimes when compared to felony burglary. If this could be done, the chief reasoned, he could go to the city council and report that *all* major crime had declined in the city during the past quarter.

The chief also mentioned in passing that he was in the process of reviewing assignments and was reconsidering whether a sergeant was needed in the crime analysis unit. In other words, change the report or be reassigned to a less-appealing job. The sergeant said he told the chief that he would review the burglary reports and get back to him. The chief told him he was doing the right thing, then shook his hand vigorously and showed him to the door.

The sergeant did review the reports as instructed by the chief. The problem was that all of them had been correctly classified as burglaries, and he would have to lie and intentionally alter police records to make the statistics reflect a reduction in burglaries. Who would know? The public wouldn't, and the FBI would review just the numbers, not the reports. The officers and civilians working for him would know, but they wanted to keep their assignments too. If he did as the chief asked, he would retain his day job with weekends off. If he didn't, he would probably be assigned to some impound lot on the graveyard shift keeping logs of towed vehicles.

The sergeant has been on the job for twenty-eight years. He has gone through four chiefs and worked the streets for most of his career. Once he had reviewed the reports and assured himself the data were correct, he submitted a written report to the chief indicating that he had reviewed the past quarter's crime statistics and all were correct. In other words, the number of burglaries would remain the same, indicating a rise in that crime category compared to the previous year. He would not lie or alter the records.

Naturally, he received no response to his memo, and it wasn't until six months later that the ax fell and he was reassigned back to the patrol division. Ethical decisions made in real life often involve unpleasant consequences. The sergeant told me that it was difficult for him to make the right choice because he could predict the ramifications, and his family liked him having a day job with weekends off. However, he also knew that if he did what the chief had asked, his entire career would have lost its meaning and he would have given away his self-respect. The sergeant had been in patrol before, and as a matter of fact he enjoyed it. The chief's "punishment" didn't work because the sergeant was at peace within himself, and the chief's approval or disapproval did not affect his self-worth. The sergeant possesses a quality of character known as virtue—the intrinsic capacity to habitually recognize and do the right thing.

At first glance, it may seem that the ethical dilemma here is caused by the sergeant's supervisor. The real conflict, however, is the sergeant's struggle to determine and do what is right, taking into consideration the ramifications his decision would have on his wife, family, and coworkers. The lesson here is that ethical behavior isn't a guarantee that others, even other members of your police department, will perceive your actions as worthy of praise. By its very definition, self-worth comes from within.

In the example, the chief didn't see changing the crime statistics as an ethical matter at all. He would argue that it's often a matter of judgment whether the elements of a crime technically define it as this type or that and that the uniform crime report definitions don't fit his particular community. Further, he would argue that reassigning the sergeant was well within his rights as chief of police. After all, he needs people in key positions who are going to "get behind him" and understand the "larger issues involved." From the chief's perspective, the sergeant wasn't being loyal to the organization. However, in his inner circle, the chief might also be heard to say that he disagrees with the sergeant and doesn't like him very much, but he does respect him. Why would the chief respect the sergeant, even though he disagrees with him and doesn't even like him? Because the sergeant acted on his convictions, even though he knew the probable consequences. The difference between the sergeant and the chief is that the sergeant reasoned through the situation from an ethical framework. The chief never gave the ethics of the matter a thought.

☯ ETHICAL DECISION MAKING IN A COMBAT ENVIRONMENT

It's even more difficult reasoning through right vs. right alternatives when you're scared, horrified, in physical danger, or disbelieving what you're seeing and hearing. On the "street," police officers see, feel, and experience things—violent death, terror, horror, and the dark side of human nature—that people living "ordinary" lives rarely experience and have virtually no frame of reference for understanding. Police officers handle unusual and emotionally charged situations involving the most personal and private aspects of people's lives. The "war on drugs," coupled with the decline of traditional societal stabilizers (family, religion, morality, and educational systems, for example), has markedly escalated the exposure of officers to traumatic experiences akin to military combat. As the causal variables of crime have increased (poverty, unemployment, underemployment, a lack of life chances, and so forth) and social stabilizers have declined, our inner cities have become battlegrounds where violence is a part of everyday life and the "norm" for increasingly larger segments of the population. Police officers are continually moving between extremes, from an "abnormal" work environment to a "normal" world of home, family, friends, organizations, and church. Over time, exposure to the type of trauma police officers encounter and the constant shifting from one world to another often have a debilitating effect on the officers' physical, spiritual, and psychological well-being. Ethical decision making often dissolves into a convenient "us vs. them" shorthand, devoid of what can be agonizing self-reflection.

After all, it's easy to act ethically when you're in pleasant surroundings, have no real time constraints, and are dealing with people you personally like and admire. It's more difficult when you're responsible for providing a "service" to people you don't like, who are obnoxious, offensive, unpleasant, and intimidating. They may also be quite different from you in terms of age, social class, ethnic background, and so on, which can add stress regardless of whether they're pleasant or unpleasant simply because of differences. The stress of having contact with these types of people causes an officer to overload emotionally, making it difficult to reason through ethical alternatives.

One of the primary difficulties associated with wearing a badge and carrying a gun that affects the ability of police officers to engage in ethical reasoning is exposure to traumatic events that have both a psychological and physical effect. For example, police officers are often exposed to such extreme job-related stresses as the victims and perpetrators of sexual assaults (adults and children), homicide and accident scenes, domestic violence, bombings and other terrorist acts, assaults on themselves, and so on. Exposure to these horrible abnormalities causes trauma and, depending on the individual officer's adaptive capacity and psychological hardiness, varying degrees of "wear and tear" to the body and mind. The "wear and tear" is often exhibited in anxiety, depression, tension, and aggression. The emotional exhaustion resulting from continual exposure to this type of stress-related trauma precipitates the changing from a positive, service-oriented, care-giving person to one who is uncaring, negative, and callous. Ethical reasoning can be suppressed by the numbness officers feel when exposed to this type of stress.

Traumatic Events Affecting Ethical Reasoning

Officer-involved shootings

Fatal traffic accidents

Special weapons and tactics (SWAT) or hostage team assignment (e.g., barricaded persons, hostage situations, and combat entry)

Serious assaults and rapes of adults and children

Narcotic unit assignment (e.g., undercover operations or search warrant combat entry)

Officer-involved hand-to-hand combat

Bomb squad assignment

Homicide investigation (e.g., deaths by violence, found bodies, terrorist acts, and autopsies)

Suicide (e.g., by hanging, shooting, or overdose)

Disasters (e.g., violent deaths by plane and train crashes, explosions, and fires)

Drive-by shootings

If the trauma is repeated often and over a long enough period of time, officers exhibit a physical and mental response commonly referred to as burnout. Officers know the stress of the job is affecting them, but they don't know what to do about it. Many adjust by using an individualized hit-or-miss system (such as exercise, meditation, or a hobby), and most officers develop healthy coping mechanisms to process these traumatic events. In a relatively short amount of time, they return to "normal" once again.

Part of this stress results from not being able to adequately help many of the victims of criminal behavior or prevent criminals from preying on the weak and helpless. What officers see and their efforts to help other people often fall short of the idealistic expectations they have established for themselves. This results in a conflict between what they would have liked to have done and what actually occurred. The loss of self-esteem resulting from failing to achieve the often superhuman goals officers set for themselves leads to depression and a sense of reduced personal accomplishment.

Adding to the constant tension of officers performing these types of jobs is the fact that their personal lives are disrupted, whether the officer is on-call or not. Having to always be ready to respond often results in an inability to fully relax and recharge emotional and physical batteries.

The types of traumatic experiences listed above, especially if they occur rapidly, cause a wound to a person's soul. Since the mind doesn't have time to process what has happened, it copes by blocking the event from the immediate thought processes so the police officer can continue to function. The wonder of the human brain is that it

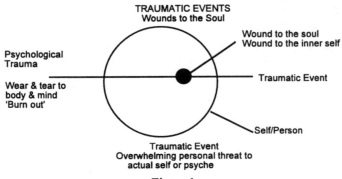

Figure 1

protects a person from consciously dealing with the enormity of what has occurred until a time when it may be psychologically safer to do so.

When too many of these types of traumatic events occur in a short amount of time, the body exhibits such symptoms as ulcers, depression, anxiety, asthma, headaches, nausea, irritability, mood swings, insomnia, and impotence. Officers who have gone through traumatic events and haven't developed the coping mechanisms or psychological hardiness developed by others experience more severe forms of stress responses (Figure 2).

Examples of these severe responses are alcoholism, drug abuse, hypertension, and suicide.

The bandage the brain places around the emotional trauma to protect the person wears off over time. As it does—often years later—the detrimental effects of suppressed emotions come out and are exhibited. Since the police culture constantly reinforces emotional hardiness as a precursor to success and often devalues therapeutic assistance, police officers suffer from the long-term detrimental effects of traumatic experiences, often dying at an early age and most often alone. When the work that police officers do drains them of their emotional energy, there is little left over for spouses, family, and friends.

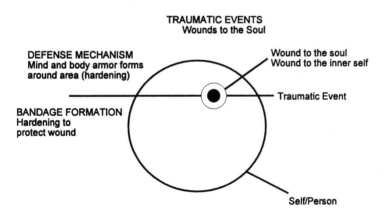

Figure 2

Many police officers I've met have become so overwhelmed by the negative side effects of doing the job that they're incapable of coping with the problems of everyday living. The irony is that somehow they can summon the inner strength to run into the flames of a burning building to save the life of a baby, but they are no longer able to do the things necessary to maintain a positive relationship with the people who love them. Except for the ability to handle emergency situations at work, they have become so angry and hostile that they can no longer provide even adequate service to the public. The police culture we spoke about earlier shields them from being fired, but it also prevents them from seeking and receiving help to deal with the problem. Most don't recognize there is a problem in the first place. An example of learning how to cope with the effects of doing the job of a police officer while retaining the strong character base needed to live in the other world of family and friends is illustrated by the following story about a friend of mine.

War Story

John Simoni is a veteran police officer who had been to countless homicide scenes and had learned how to detach himself from what he was seeing and doing. This time, however, the situation was complicated by the arrival of a high-ranking police official. Since John had been the first officer at the scene, he had been given the tedious task of keeping a log of everyone who entered the crime scene. When the captain arrived, John dutifully wrote his name and time of arrival on the log. The captain was inside for about twenty minutes, and when he came out he was carrying a large paper grocery bag, which appeared to be quite full. The captain hadn't been carrying the bag when he entered the crime scene.

As John began writing down the time of the captain's departure, the captain put the bag down on the front step and said, "Let me have a look at that log."

Thinking he wanted to inspect it, John handed it over. Instead, the captain took out a felt-tipped pen and carefully blocked out his name saying, "I was never here. You never saw me. Do you understand?"

The captain was a powerful man in the police department, and John knew he had destroyed the careers of several officers who had gone against his wishes.

Bewildered, John nodded his assent to the captain, who patted him on the shoulder, picked up the grocery bag, and as he was leaving commanded, "Leave my name out of your written report."

As a veteran officer, John knew the captain's name should be recorded on the crime scene log. He knew he would be attesting on his written report that he had, in fact, logged everyone in and out of the crime scene. He didn't know what the captain had placed in the bag. Was it evidence? The victim's personal belongings? He did catch part of a conversation between two detectives indicating that the captain had known the murder victim. To complicate matters further, John was first on the promotion list to detective, and he knew how easy it would be for the captain to block any chances he might have.

John assessed his alternatives. Who other than he would know or care whether the captain's name was placed on the log? If anyone questioned him, he could always say so many people were entering and leaving the crime scene that he had made an honest mistake. What the captain had in the paper bag was none of his business, and besides, he honestly didn't know what was in it.

He would have to lie, of course. He would have to lie on his report by omitting information, and there was a chance that he might have to go to court and lie there too.

John wrote the captain's name in large block letters on the crime scene log, right below the place where the captain had blocked his name out, and inserted the correct times of his arrival and departure. He submitted his report indicating that he had recorded the names and time of all who had entered and exited the crime scene. He did not mention the bag the captain was carrying when he left the scene, but he knew there was a good chance someone would eventually question him about it. When they did, he would tell the truth.

Being an honorable man, there was only one thing remaining for Simoni to do. He telephoned the captain and told him he had put his name on the log. The captain hung up on him. This probably meant he could kiss his gold detective's badge good-bye, along with the increase in salary and prestige that went with it. He would most likely end up walking a beat on the midnight shift for an extended period of time.

After his shift, when John arrived at home, his wife told him that the clothes dryer was broken, there was water in the basement again, and his son had gotten another detention at school. This is John's "other" world. He went down the basement and lifted weights for an hour, sloshing around in the water, taking his anxieties out on the weight stack. He was hurting, but his efforts to contain his emotions and his machismo prevented him from talking to his wife about why just then. She knew that eventually John would tell her what was wrong and allow her to help.

John felt he had made the right decision and was prepared to pay the consequences for it. He emerged from the basement, gave his wife a water soaked hug, and he and his son began fixing the broken dryer. John listened while his son crafted a neat defense as to why he had pulled the pigtail of the girl sitting in front of him, who just happened to be the principal's daughter. John was doing the things necessary to heal himself emotionally, and for him it was just a matter of time before his batteries would be recharged.

The point here is that many officers don't have John's inner strength or support structure to help make the transition between what is seen at work and what others consider to be normal everyday living. We become burned out, drained by the emotional energy required to wear a badge and carry a gun, and less willing to share what energy we have left with others. Many police officers refuse to talk about the job with the people who care about them, rationalizing that they are protecting their families and friends from the harsh realities of the world they work in. However, what's really occurring is that the officers are trying to protect themselves from having to relive the pain of the emotional trauma that the experiences produced.

Consider the following symptoms of burnout and their effect on a person's ability to resolve complicated ethical dilemmas:

- A sense of limited ability to accomplish persona and professional goals

- Loss of self-esteem caused by unreasonable expectations for self and others

- Reduced motivation

- Increased frustration

- Doing the bare minimum and going strictly by the book

- Preferring things rather than people and treating people as obstacles rather than fellow human beings

- Avoiding eye contact or physical contact (even a handshake) with members of the public

- Never smiling and giving no reply to questions or answering only with a grunt

It's very difficult to sustain the inner strength necessary to do the job required of a police officer. The hardest part of it is that you have to do it every day. Those with a clear set of values and ethics adopt a philosophy of life enabling them to withstand the tremendous negative pressures faced by today's officers.

Character is made by what you stand for; reputation,
by what you fall for.

Robert Quinlin

☯ POLICE DISCRETION: IMPACT ON OFFICER ETHICS

The policeman (or woman) on the beat or in the patrol car makes more decisions and exercises broader discretion affecting the daily lives of people every day and to a greater extent, in many respects, than a judge will ordinarily exercise in a week.

Chief Justice Warren Burger

To further understand why police ethics are considered by society and the police profession to be so important, consider the following statement and its moral and ethical implications: *The individual police officer has more inherent discretionary power than any other single person in American society.* Contrary to the assumption of many people that the police have no discretion and function in strict accordance with the rules of law, most police behavior is the result of interpretation by the individual officer about what should or should not be done.

As pointed out by the late O.W. Wilson, who is widely regarded as the greatest authority on police administration, "the traditional American response to any offensive behavior has been the enactment of a law against it, with the result that the statute books and city ordinances are filled up with prohibitions against conduct that many persons have come to regard as innocuous" (Wilson 1977). If the police rigidly enforced every law, statute, and ordinance, the criminal justice system would come to a grinding halt. The experienced law enforcement officer balances the interests of the community as a whole with the individual interests of its citizens in enforcing the law. If this were not the case, a doctor driving a few miles an hour over the speed limit to get to the hospital for an emergency would be detained and cited for speeding, and every loud public argument would result in arrests for breach of peace.

Police officers, under certain circumstances, have the right to kill. They have the right to detain and deprive people of their liberty through arrest and detainment. Even in a democracy, the exercise of these enormous powers often occurs without prior judicial review or approval and is based solely on an officer interpreting a situation, weighing the alternatives, and deciding on the proper course of action. In situations involving the use of deadly physical force by a police officer, there is no trial, judge, or jury of the person's peers. Furthermore, the exercise of these powers by a police officer most often occurs without even the guidance of a police department supervisor. It is solely dependent on the officer's ability to apply accumulated knowledge, experience, and judgment to difficult legal and ethical dilemmas.

In addition, police officers make decisions every single work day about which laws to enforce or not enforce and when, who to arrest and who to let go, whether to warn or issue a ticket, and how much force to use when effecting an arrest. Police officers make discretionary decisions as to when it is appropriate to search people, their cars, and their homes. Studies indicate that the majority of arrests made by the police occur without an arrest warrant signed by a judge and are based on an officer's perception of whether probable cause to arrest exists. The individual police officer weighs the alternatives and makes these independent decisions on the street under very dangerous and stressful conditions without the benefit of law books or scarcely even time for reflection.

Unlike most organizations, it is the individual police officers at the bottom of the organization's hierarchy who have the most discretion in decision making. They are the ones who decide whether to apply the law. When one considers the fact that there are approximately seventeen thousand law enforcement agencies in the United States employing more than eight hundred thousand people, the magnitude of the daily decision-making process becomes impressive (U.S. Dept. of Justice 1988).

This discretionary decision making by the individual police officer walking a beat or patrolling in a vehicle occurs in an environment as alien to the average person as the surface of the moon. Policing occurs in a world peopled by predators, drug dealers, pimps, prostitutes, murderers, and rapists: people who not only have no ethics, but also have no conscience and will hurt other people and never give the right or wrong of it a second thought. Police officers see all the unimaginable horror that human beings are capable of committing. They work in an environment permeated by corruption, where officers are continuously exposed to temptations and opportunities most people only read about in what they think is fiction.

The extraordinary diversity of American urban society is itself a variable affecting police officer ethics. A study by Jody Klein and Douglas Smith found that the police use formal arrest procedures more often in lower class than in middle and upper class neighborhoods (Klein 1984). As the agency of last resort, the police constantly deal with the most dangerous side of human nature in the desperate, the down-trodden, and the physically and mentally ill. To expect this not to have an effect on an officer's ability to reason through ethical alternatives is unrealistic.

Many forms of police discretion involve ethical decisions relative to the use of police powers, even in routine calls for service. Consider the following routine call. See if you can pick out areas involving police discretion and matters of ethics. Do you approve or disapprove of the actions and behaviors of the officers? A discussion of the pertinent sections follows the reading passage.

War Story

A Routine Call

Officer John Anderson has been a member of the police department for the past five years. He is assigned to a police district located principally in and around a housing project. The majority of the residents of the housing project are unemployed. The area has a very high crime rate, and street sales of narcotics have reached open-market proportions. It is July, and Officer Anderson is working the 4:00 P.M. to 12:00 A.M. shift. At 7:20 P.M., he receives a radio call from the police dispatcher to respond to 221 Bellevue Street, Apartment 3D, on a report from a citizen of a domestic dispute. Another police officer, Mike Bellini, is also dispatched as a backup.

Officer Anderson has been to the address before and knows that Paul and Evelyn Foster live there. He has arrested Mr. Foster twice this month for assaulting his wife. Anderson radios Officer Bellini and learns that it will be about ten minutes before he can meet Anderson at the scene. As Officer Anderson is making his way through traffic, he is informed by the dispatcher that two additional calls have now been received relative to a domestic dispute at the apartment. Anderson switches on his vehicle's red lights and siren and speeds to the scene, going through several stop signs and red traffic lights after brief pauses to make certain it was safe to do so. Finding no place to park when he reaches the apartment complex, he double-parks in the street. Anderson quickly exits the vehicle and hurries toward the apartment building, but stops, remembering that Mr. Foster is six five, weighs 245, and has a history of resisting arrest. He radios Officer Bellini again and learns that he is now only about three minutes away. Officer Anderson ascends the steps leading up to the third floor apartment while listening and looking for signs of danger from above. Upon reaching the third floor, he hears two shouting voices inside 3D and walks over to listen at the apartment's door. Silence, then shouted arguing again. Officer Bellini radios that he is downstairs and on the way up.

Once joined by Officer Bellini, Anderson knocks firmly on the door, then loudly states, "Police officers. Open up."

There is no response, but the officers can hear the argument continuing inside the apartment.

After a few moments, Anderson raps on the door with his metal flashlight and shouts, "This is the police. We have a complaint about the noise. Open up the goddamn door right now, or we'll break it down."

Still no response from inside, but the arguing grows louder, and the officers hear a woman scream in the apartment. Officer Anderson tries the door and to their surprise it is unlocked. Both officers enter the apartment directly into the living room. They see a portable television with a broken screen lying on the floor and an overturned end table.

Mr. Foster suddenly storms out of the bedroom yelling, "Who the fuck let you in here? We didn't call the police. Get the fuck out!"

Foster, dressed only in a pair of undershorts, advances on the officers, shouting obscenities, fists ready to fly.

Officer Anderson takes out his nightstick and points it at Foster, yelling back, "Shut the fuck up and sit down. Where is your wife?"

At the same time, Officer Bellini moves toward the bedroom. Foster steps past Anderson and blocks Bellini's path.

"You got no right storming in here without no warrant or nothing and bothering folk! Get the fuck out of here!"

Bellini screams back at Foster, "If you don't want to spend the night in the hospital, you'd better get out of my fucking face!"

At this point, Anderson grabs Foster by the arm and yells, "Now sit the fuck down on the sofa, or you're under arrest."

Foster sits down but continues shouting a string of obscenities at both officers. Bellini enters the bedroom where he finds Mrs. Foster sitting on the bed, bleeding from a cut to her lip.

"What happened to your face?" Bellini asks.

Mrs. Foster shrugs.

"It was an accident. I hit it on the closet door. What are you doing here? I didn't call the police."

"Your neighbors called about the noise. Your husband hit you, didn't he?" Bellini asks.

The woman looked very frightened. "No, he didn't hit me. I cut my lip on the closet door."

She starts to get up, but Bellini stops her. "Sit the fuck back down until I'm through talking. Now you both can go to jail for breach of peace, or you can tell the truth and we'll lock your asshole husband up. It doesn't matter to me. Which is it?"

Mrs. Foster knew that if her husband was arrested he would be out on bond and back within a few hours.

"I don't know nothing," she says.

Bellini instructs Mrs. Foster not to move from the bed or she will be arrested, and he rejoins Anderson in the living room, telling him about Mrs. Foster's cut lip.

Anderson has better luck with Mr. Foster.

"Why did you hit your wife?" he asks.

Foster suddenly gets up from the sofa and shouts, "Because I caught her fucking with another guy! OK?"

"You're under arrest," Anderson says, and he and Bellini handcuff Foster.

He does not resist but says, "Let me at least put some fucking clothes on before you bring me outside."

Anderson and Bellini consider Foster's request for a moment, knowing they were lucky to get him in handcuffs in the first place. They help him find a pair of shorts and sneakers and get them on him. No shirt though. That would mean having to take the cuffs off.

Bellini tells Mrs. Foster that her husband has admitted to assaulting her and has been placed under arrest, and he explains the various services the state offers to battered women. She declines any offer for assistance but asks how long it will be before her husband gets out of jail.

Bellini responds, "Beats me. I only lock 'em up. I don't make the laws; I only enforce them."

A crowd gathers as Mr. Foster is brought out of the building and placed in the back seat of Anderson's patrol car. Anderson has decided to transport Foster to the station himself rather than call for the paddy wagon to come get him.

Several hours later, Anderson writes a report about Mr. Foster's arrest. The total amount of time Officers Anderson and Bellini were in Mr. and Mrs. Foster's apartment was seven minutes.

Many police officers from all across the country fail to see the ways in which such situations as the routine call above involve ethical decisions. That's because rationalizing that an officer's action (or inaction) was "legal" or "department policy" and did not call for moral judgment is easier than facing tough ethical questions. By rationalizing, officers remove themselves from even asking "What is the right thing to do?" and make no critical assessment of their own behavior. The type of critical assessment required to be ethical involves disciplining oneself to review personal actions and making a determination of whether behavior has been ethical. This type of review may be painful because officers may recognize that they have fallen short of the expectations they set for themselves. However, the ability to think through one's behavior for the purpose of changing it is what sets us apart as human beings.

Following is a discussion of the situations in the routine call that involved ethical decision making. In thinking about these discretionary and ethical decisions, ask yourself the following questions:

● Are the officers' actions legal?

● Are the officers' actions ethical—the right thing to do—under the circumstances?

● Are any of the behaviors exhibited by the officers unethical? If so, why?

1. *Anderson switches on his vehicle's red lights and siren and speeds to the scene, going through several stop signs and red traffic lights after brief pauses to make certain it was safe to do so.*

Discussion

The officer uses his judgment, based on training, experience, and knowledge of the law, to determine how important it is to get to the scene quickly, whether to invoke police powers by using the vehicle's red lights and siren, and the benefits vs. danger to the community of going through stop signs and red lights. All states have statutes defining when a police cruiser is considered to be an "emergency vehicle," and most departments have guidelines for engaging a cruiser's red lights and siren. However, from a practical standpoint, the decision as to when and how best to get to a scene is left to the officer.

The point in this discussion is not whether the officer has a legal right to inconvenience and cause anxiety to other motorists, but whether he gave any thought to the fact that he is invoking the enormous powers of the government the moment the button is pushed or switch flipped to turn on the lights and siren, while other drivers pull to the curb to allow him to pass.

2. *Finding no place to park when he reaches the apartment complex, he double-parks in the street.*

Discussion

The officer determines that double-parking in the street, which he routinely gives others tickets for doing, is permissible because of the nature of the police call. When we see a police cruiser illegally parked, we assume that an emergency requires an officer's immediate presence. The point here is whether the officer fully understands that society allows this parking inconvenience for the express purpose of allowing the police to respond quickly to an emergency situation.

3. *Anderson quickly exits the vehicle and hurries toward the apartment building, but stops, remembering that Mr. Foster is six five, weighs 245, and has a history of resisting arrest.*

Discussion

The officer decides when it's important to move rapidly and whether to wait for an assisting officer. He makes this decision based on his perception of the threat of danger to himself and others. Even though the officer has used the police vehicle's red lights and siren to get to the scene quickly and has double-parked in the street, there is nothing wrong with thinking through the situation and waiting for more police officers.

4. *Once joined by Officer Bellini, Anderson knocks firmly on the door, then loudly states, "Police officers. Open up."*

   There is no response, but the officers can hear the argument continuing inside the apartment.

   After a few moments, Anderson raps on the door with his metal flashlight and shouts, "This is the police. We have a complaint about the noise. Open up the goddamn door right now, or we'll break it down."

Discussion

The officers decide how and when to announce the presence of the police, what tone of voice to use, and what type of language is appropriate based on the law, the sum of their experience, knowledge about the type of call, and previous dealings with Mr. and Mrs. Foster. The officers also decide when it is appropriate to threaten the use of force.

We are informed in the opening paragraph that the apartment is located in a housing project where most of the people are unemployed and crime is high. We also know that Officer Anderson has been to the location in the past and has already arrested Mr. Foster twice this month for assaulting his wife. Still, would Anderson "rap on the door with his metal flashlight" if he were a police officer in a quiet suburban community and he was standing at the door of a $300,000 home situated at the end of a picturesque driveway? Using the flashlight as a door knocker is inappropriate. In the suburban setting, would the officer use language such as "Open up the goddamn door right now, or we'll break it down!"? If the answer is no, why then would the officer's behavior be acceptable in this situation? Use of profanity by police officers is always wrong.

5. *Still no response from inside, but the arguing grows louder, and the officers hear a woman scream in the apartment. Officer Anderson tries the door and to their surprise it is unlocked. Both officers enter the apartment directly into the living room.*

Discussion

The officers decide how to interpret the Fourth Amendment in this situation, what the exigent circumstances are, whether a crime is being committed, what the scream means, and whether to obtain a search warrant prior to entering. The purpose of these sentences is to illustrate that these types of decisions are made in a split second without the luxury of looking up court decisions on such esoteric terms as "probable cause," Fourth Amendment exceptions to search warrants, "lawful entry," and "exigent circumstances." In most states, police officers can enter premises without a warrant if they have probable cause to believe a felony is being committed inside, and they have announced themselves as police officers but have been denied entry.

6. *They see a portable television with a broken screen lying on the floor and an overturned end table.*

   Mr. Foster suddenly storms out of the bedroom yelling, "Who the fuck let you in here? We didn't call the police. Get the fuck out."

   Foster, dressed only in a pair of undershorts, advances on the officers, shouting obscenities, fists ready to fly.

Officer Anderson takes out his nightstick and points it at Foster, yelling back, "Shut the fuck up and sit down. Where is your wife?"

At the same time, Officer Bellini moves toward the bedroom. Foster steps past Anderson and blocks Bellini's path.

"You got no right storming in here without no warrant or nothing and bothering folk! Get the fuck out of here!"

Bellini screams back at Foster, "If you don't want to spend the night in the hospital, you'd better get out of my fucking face!"

At this point, Anderson grabs Foster by the arm and yells, "Now sit the fuck down on the sofa, or you're under arrest."

Foster sits down but continues shouting a string of obscenities at both officers.

Discussion

The officers decide when Mr. Foster can speak in his own home, when he can and cannot move, and whether he shall sit or stand. They also choose the type of verbal communication and body language they will use in controlling Mr. Foster's movements. They accomplish this control partially through the implied use of a deadly weapon for noncompliance and by physically taking hold of Mr. Foster. Although the language used by the officers is inappropriate, they certainly have an obligation to determine if Mrs. Foster is OK. However, unless Mr. Foster is under arrest for committing a crime, using force to make him sit down is wrong. Using obscenities and yelling at police officers in your own home is not unlawful.

7.   *Bellini enters the bedroom where he finds Mrs. Foster sitting on the bed, bleeding from a cut to her lip.*

"What happened to your face?" Bellini asks.

Mrs. Foster shrugs.

"*It was an accident. I hit it on the closet door. What are you doing here? I didn't call the police.*"

"*Your neighbors called about the noise. Your husband hit you, didn't he?*" *Bellini asks.*

The woman looked very frightened. "*No, he didn't hit me. I cut my lip on the closet door.*"

She starts to get up, but Bellini stops her. "*Sit the fuck back down until I'm through talking. Now you both can go to jail for breach of peace, or you can tell the truth and we'll lock your asshole husband up. It doesn't matter to me. Which is it?*"

Mrs. Foster knew that if her husband was arrested he would be out on bond and back within a few hours.

"*I don't know nothing,*" *she says.*

Bellini instructs Mrs. Foster not to move from the bed or she will be arrested, and he rejoins Anderson in the living room, telling him about Mrs. Foster's cut lip.

 Discussion

Officer Bellini decides how to communicate with Mrs. Foster, what language to use, what questions to ask, what questions to not ask, whether to allow her to sit or stand, where she can sit or stand, and whether to believe or not believe what she is telling him. An implied threat of arrest is also used in this "interview." The officer must interview Mrs. Foster to determine if she needs medical attention and whether a crime has been committed; however, the language the officer uses, his threat of arrest, and the controlling of her movements are all an abuse of police power and are unethical.

8. *Anderson has better luck with Mr. Foster.*

    "Why did you hit your wife?" he asks.

    Foster suddenly gets up from the sofa and screams, "Because I caught her fucking with another guy! OK?"

    "You're under arrest," Anderson says, and he and Bellini handcuff Foster.

    He does not resist but says, "Let me at least put some fucking clothes on before you bring me outside."

Discussion

The officer decides whether to advise Foster of his constitutional right against self-incrimination. He also chooses the types of questions to ask, chooses to not ask some questions, determines when probable cause has been established, and decides whether to arrest, to warn, to refer to another agency, or do nothing.

The officers were required to advise Mr. Foster of his constitutional right against self-incrimination. They did not. There is no complaint from Mrs. Foster. She denies being assaulted by her husband, and she says she accidentally cut her lip on the closet door. Other than his admission to the officers that he struck his wife, what criminal case is there against Mr. Foster? Will the officers lie on their report by stating that after advising Mr. Foster of his constitutional right to remain silent and have an attorney present before questioning him that he freely admitted to criminally assaulting his wife? An ethical dilemma is clearly present.

9. *Anderson and Bellini consider Foster's request for a moment, knowing they were lucky to get him in handcuffs in the first place. They help him find a pair of shorts and sneakers and get them on him. No shirt though. That would mean having to take the cuffs off.*

Discussion

Even with a department rule about handcuffing prisoners, the officers still decide whether to handcuff, when in the process to handcuff, whether to let Mr. Foster—now a prisoner—wear clothing and of what type, and how much assistance to give him in dressing. The officers are correct to make a good faith judgment on their ability to control Mr. Foster if they remove the handcuffs.

10. *Bellini tells Mrs. Foster that her husband has admitted to assaulting her and has been placed under arrest, and he explains the various services the state offers to battered women. She declines any offer for assistance but asks how long it will be before her husband gets out of jail.*

   Bellini responds, "Beats me. I only lock 'em up. I don't make the laws; I only enforce them."

Discussion

The officers decide whether to arrest Mrs. Foster along with her husband, what information to give or withhold, and what role they will assume in protecting Mrs. Foster after her husband is released.

11. *A crowd gathers as Mr. Foster is brought out of the building and placed in the back seat of Anderson's patrol car. Anderson had decided to transport Foster to the station himself rather than call for the paddy wagon to come get him.*

   Several hours later, Anderson writes a report about Mr. Foster's arrest. The total amount of time Officers Anderson and Bellini were in Mr. and Mrs. Foster's apartment was seven minutes.

Discussion

The officers decide what happens to Mr. Foster after his arrest, how long the arrest process will take, and what to include or not include in the written report.

We are also informed that the total amount of time the officers were in the Fosters' apartment was seven minutes. Consider the number of ethical decisions the officers made, or neglected to make, in those seven minutes.

It should be obvious by now that police officers have difficult ethical choices even when acting under the authority of law and departmental rules and regulations. Experienced police officers use these enormous police powers almost automatically and often in a split second. They engage their cruisers' red lights and sirens to get through traffic in order to respond to calls; decide whether and when to enter private property; tell people to sit, stand, or move; select language appropriate for various situations; decide when to threaten or use force, and so on. However, over time, the consequences of making these types of decisions may have lasting effects on the officers and the people they come into contact with. Those officers who rationalize away their individual morality, ethics, and personal responsibility are more apt to suffer the debilitating psychological and physiological effects so common to today's officers: posttraumatic stress syndrome, alcoholism, marital dysfunction, high blood pressure, heart disease, depression, and even suicide.

"To educate a person in mind and not in morals is to educate a menace to society."

Theodore Roosevelt

☯ ORGANIZATIONAL EFFECT ON POLICE ETHICS

In policing, it is the subtler forms of unethical behavior that most often fail to be corrected because of a perception on the part of police supervisors and managers that an officer's "intentions" or "motives" were good. A response to poor behavior that's been around policing for many years is the question "Was it a mistake of the heart or a mistake of the head?" Mistakes of the heart are dealt with much more leniently than mistakes of the head, which are actions an officer knew or should have known were wrong. Wrongdoing was covered in the list on page 12. Here is an example of a mistake of the heart.

War Story

A national newspaper recently featured an article about community-oriented policing in a city with a significant crime problem. The usual sociological factors over which the police have no control—unemployment, gang affiliation, poverty, and homelessness—were mentioned. The story was written by a reporter who had ridden along with a "veteran" officer (three years on the job) as he responded to calls in what was described as a "rough neighborhood." The reporter was also with the officer as he made the rounds of restaurants that "cater to the police," receiving free food and coffee that the officer then delivered to homeless people. A photo with the caption "community-oriented policing" showed the officer drinking a cup of the free coffee with a homeless person, obviously a prostitute, who grinned happily for the photographer. The objective of the article was to explain community-oriented policing and the improved relations between the police and the community.

I cringed as I read the article and looked at the photograph. Are you wondering why? If you are, then it's good you're reading this book. First, I'm not sure what "catering to the police" is, but I have a pretty good idea that it means they provide officers with gratuities.

More importantly, it's obvious that neither the police officer nor the reporter had a clue that the actions and behavior of the officer were *wrong*. Obtaining "free food and coffee," regardless of what his motive may have been, was wrong. This is a classic example of trying to do the right thing in the wrong way. Did the customers in the restaurants that "cater to the police," who saw the officer walking out with free food and coffee, know he was giving it to the homeless? Or, did they just see an officer not paying for his food? Even if the customers knew the free food and coffee was not for the officer but for the homeless, were his actions a proper use of his badge of office? Was the behavior OK as long as the officer's "intentions" were good? Who is he harming? He is harming everyone who wears a badge and the community he serves.

Now, if the officer got in line like everyone else, ordered the food and coffee like everyone else, paid for it like everyone else, and then gave it to the homeless without anyone but the recipients knowing, it would then become the act of a *warrior* and worthy of admiration. Anything less is an abuse of power, unethical, and perhaps even a form of graft.

What makes this event appalling is that the officer felt comfortable enough with what he was doing to showcase his actions as worthy of praise. I wonder if this officer has a mentor in his police department, someone he respects, who could approach him and say, "You did a nice job with that reporter and the piece on community-oriented policing. But there's another way to look at it, a different perspective that you may want to consider." A mentor might use words like this to explain to the officer that although his intentions were admirable, the methods he used to accomplish them were not and why. This officer's heart was in the right place, he just didn't have enough experience to appreciate how his actions might be perceived by others.

War Story

Another example illustrates a mistake of the heart made by a veteran officer who should have known better. I recently rode with a police sergeant in one of our nation's largest cities. A call came in over the police radio about a felony just a few blocks from where we were parked having our coffee. It was a report of shots having been fired, and it was unknown if anyone was hit. Since there was no reaction from the sergeant, I asked him if we would be going to the call.

His answer was, "Oh, we don't go into the projects after dark. That's gang territory. It's too dangerous. If more calls come in, and if someone is actually shot, then we'll get enough cops together and go in."

He said this matter-of-factly, as if everyone knew this but me. I said, "What do you mean you don't go? You're a cop. We always go!"

He looked at me as if I were crazy and said, "Larry, you've been off the streets too long. It's not the same as it was years ago when you were a cop."

To top it all off, he made this statement with a great deal of confidence, as if it was an undisputed fact that police officers respond only when the odds are on their side. I was astonished and deeply saddened. When the cops are afraid to go, or don't care, we are in deep trouble! As Edmund Burke said, "All that is essential for the triumph of evil is that good men do nothing."

My experience with this sergeant was an isolated incident. He was a burned-out cop who no longer cared. While he was telling me that it was too dangerous for the police to go into the projects after dark, the radio was chattering away about officers who had already arrived at the scene of the shooting and had a suspect in custody. The sergeant must have figured I no longer knew how to interpret the cryptic messages coming over the police radio.

When I pointed out to him that his officers had already responded and captured a suspect, he grinned sheepishly and said, "Well, I guess it's safe, so we can take a ride over there."

The sergeant no longer had the heart for the job. He was close to retirement, and it was obvious he didn't want to take any chances that he might be called on to make a supervisory decision. His actions were a mistake of the heart and unethical.

You and I know that the vast majority of police officers are honest, hardworking, and brave. Some police officer somewhere is saving a life, investigating a robbery, or preventing a crime from happening as you read these words. They're doing a job that can best be described as working in a war zone armed with a pea shooter and restricted by rules that only they have to obey. Police officers perform acts of courage and devotion to duty all the time. But the job is performed in an environment requiring such a high degree of psychological hardiness that it cannot help but have a negative effect on a person. This coupled with the fact that discretionary power lends itself to abuse is precisely why a strong ethical base is necessary.

☯ TEN ETHICAL DILEMMAS FACING POLICE OFFICERS

The following are ethical dilemmas that police officers face every day. When reading the cases that follow, consider the following questions:

1. What are the ethical dilemmas in each scenario?

2. What legal issues are involved, and should they play a role in making ethical decisions?

3. What are the consequences of choosing to act or not act in each situation?

4. On what are you basing your decision? social contract ethics? rule ethics? individual ethics? a combination of all three?

5. What criterion or standard are you using to justify whether your actions are "good," "bad," "ethical," or "unethical"?

1. Whether to sustain life or allow a person to die

You are a police officer walking a beat in the downtown section of a large city. There is an alley where the homeless have erected small tent-like structures for sleeping in and storing their meager possessions. It is an area peopled by the destitute, the alcoholic, the addicted, and the mentally ill. The alley has been an informal home to the homeless for many years, and although complaints have been lodged about the people living there, no "official" action has ever been taken. You have made it a practice to routinely walk through the alley several times during your tour of duty to make certain everything is "OK."

It's 9:00 P.M. in the middle of summer. While making your way through the alley, your flashlight beams across an old man, perhaps in his seventies, lying face down next to a dumpster. You find that he is barely alive, has defecated and vomited all over himself, and is going through the last stages of delirium tremens. When you turn him over, you recognize he is a "police regular" and remember that he has AIDS. The old man suddenly stops breathing and begins turning blue. You radio for a police cruiser with portable oxygen, but are informed it will be about five minutes before the closest police unit can get there. An ambulance will take even longer.

Knowing the man has AIDS, do you give him cardiopulmonary resuscitation (CPR) and risk the possibility of becoming infected, or do you allow him to die?

 Discussion

This scenario presents a difficult dilemma for the officer. Either decision—choosing to administer unprotected CPR on a person known to have AIDS, or choosing to do nothing and allowing the man to die—has significant consequences. Providing unprotected CPR on a person with AIDS exposes the officer to high risk of contracting a disease which could ultimately result in the officer's death. The ramifications of making the choice to act might have horrible consequences for the officer, the department, and his or her family.

Choosing **not** to administer unprotected CPR to a person known to have AIDS also may result in consequences for the officer, the department and, of course, the man who has stopped breathing. Depending on the individual officer he or she might spend a considerable length of time after the event revisiting the decision trying to figure out what would have been the "right" thing to do. There may also be legal ramifications in choosing not to act depending on the laws of your individual state and, of course, the inevitable civil suit.

However, the ethical dilemma posed here is: "How far should a police officer be expected to go to save the life of another?" What method should be used to determine the answer to this question and who should be the final authority? The courts? The officer? The department? Do we use the legal "reasonable and prudent standard" in determining whether the officer's decision was right or wrong or are these types of decisions best left to the officer's individual discretion and moral code? Is the decision-making process in this scenario different from that of a police officer who chooses to risk his life to run into a burning building to rescue a child? What if this were your wife, father, or mother? If it wasn't a stranger, but someone you loved, would you then expect the officer to give unprotected CPR?

What would you do? Why?

2. Whether to obey orders you think are illegal

You and several other police officers are dispatched to the scene of a "disturbance" at a clinic where abortions are performed. It is Sunday, and the clinic is closed. Upon arriving at the scene, you observe ten people walking up and down the sidewalk in front of the clinic saying the rosary. The group is being led by a Catholic priest. You are a Christian and would describe yourself as "pro-life." A police sergeant at the scene orders you and the other officers to arrest the "protesters" for creating a "breach of peace." The protesters are on public property, not blocking anyone's entrance or egress to the clinic, and there is no court order prohibiting their protest. You approach the sergeant and ask her what crime the people are committing. You point out that they are on public property, are continuously moving and not blocking anyone's entrance or exit, the clinic is closed, and no one to your knowledge has made a complaint. You ask if there is a court order. The sergeant points to her stripes and says, "This is all you need to know. Now arrest those people, or I'll have you walking a beat for the rest of your life."

What would you do?

Discussion

Failure by a police officer to obey the lawful orders of a supervisor is a violation of rules and regulations in all police departments. It would be rare indeed for a police officer in the above situation not to follow the sergeant's orders. Obviously, the key words here are "lawful orders." There may, in fact, be a court order prohibiting the protesters from being where they are. The sergeant isn't required to explain this to the officer. If time permitted, it would be good supervision to answer the officer's questions and explain why arrests must be made. However, the sergeant isn't required to do so, nor is she required to obtain consensus from all of the officers present as to what should be done. The sergeant is not directing the officer to act unethically or illegally by beating the protesters, writing false information in a report, or destroying evidence, for example. The officers are being directed to take the protesters into custody to be brought before a court to answer for a crime they are alleged to have committed.

The officer is free to question the sergeant again later, take the matter up with the sergeant's supervisor, determine if an order from a court did exist, prefer disciplinary action against the sergeant, and write factual information relative to the situation in a report. The fact that the officer may have a great deal of respect for the priest leading the protesters, is a Christian, "pro-life," thinks the protesters are "right," and may not like the way the sergeant spoke, should not confuse the real ethical issue involved. It may be that the officer's personal values and beliefs are in conflict with the action required of a police officer. This then requires the officer to reason through his or her ethical value system, sifting the pros and cons of different courses of action, and following the course of conduct with the most "rightness" attached to it.

3. To kill or not to kill

A. You are the first police officer to arrive at a crime scene where a ten-year-old child has shot and killed his father with a bolt-action rifle. The scene is an apartment located in a housing complex. The father had stabbed his wife with a kitchen knife, and she is lying semiconscious on the kitchen floor, bleeding profusely from a wound to her chest. The child has assumed a protective stance over his mother's body and is pointing the rifle at you, threatening to shoot if you come any closer. You see the child's finger is on the trigger. You try talking to the child, but he doesn't respond. Your weapon is drawn.

What would you do?

B.   Consider another ten-year-old child. He is a passenger in a stolen car you are chasing. The car comes to a screeching stop, the doors open, and all of the occupants bail out. You leap out of your patrol car and chase them down an alley. At a high chain-link fence, you come upon the ten-year-old. He turns with a gun in his hands and points it at you. Your gun is drawn.

What would you do?

Discussion

There is no definitive answer to either of these situations. It's difficult to say what the right action is in a combat situation. We know that in every state, the law gives an officer the legal right to use deadly physical force when all other means have failed and the officer or another person is in imminent danger of being killed. However, knowing what is the right thing to do is easier when you're protecting someone other than yourself. In both of these cases, there is no third person. It's between the officer and a child holding a rifle or gun. If this were a movie scene, the officer would holster his or her weapon to show the child that no harm would come to him, the child would fire anyway, and somehow the wounded officer would close the distance and manage to wrestle the firearm from the child.

In real life, perhaps the best we can expect is that the officer will try anything and everything within his or her power so as not to have to take the life of another person. It is ethical to shoot if you think the child is about to kill you. Is it more ethical not to shoot and be killed? There are components of rightness to both decisions—and all of the alternatives that may lie between those two extremes. My personal ethical view is a hope that in each of these two cases, I would have the fortitude to not fire my weapon unless the child made a further indication beyond pointing the weapon at me that I was about to die.

4.   Whether to arrest, warn, or do nothing

You have been assigned to the same area of the city for the past three years. An aging prostitute, known to you and the rest of the department for many years, is on the corner plying her trade. You know she is addicted to heroin and is dying from leukemia. She can barely stand. You observe her approach a vehicle to negotiate a price. She gets in and the vehicle pulls off.

Would you stop the vehicle for further investigation? If so, would you give a warning to both driver and prostitute? Would you allow the driver to leave and admonish the prostitute to "get out of the area"? Or would you do nothing? Would you follow the car at a discreet distance until more probable cause factors are present? If so, what if you actually saw money exchange hands and significant steps in committing the crime of prostitution begin to take place? Would you arrest the woman? the man? warn both? Allow the man to leave, but arrest the woman? Arrest no one, but tell the prostitute she is required to "find out" some information for you which may lead to solving a more important crime? What would you do?

Discussion

Sometimes the right thing to do is reason through the alternatives and choose to do nothing. This is not one of those times. Two sentences are the key to knowing the right action in this situation: "You know she is addicted to heroin and is dying from leukemia. She can barely stand." The right thing to do is get the woman medical treatment. If you're convinced her illness has left her incapable of caring for herself, then in most states you can take her into custody and transport her to a hospital without technically arresting her. Could you place her under arrest? Of course, but the criminal part of her conduct is only a consideration in that if you arrest her, it will allow you to see that she gets medical treatment, even if it is against her express wishes.

What is the right thing to do with her customer? Arrest him or warn him? Both courses of action have components of rightness attached to them. If you arrested her (even if it was to facilitate medical treatment), then based on the information given, there is probable cause to arrest him for patronizing a prostitute. If you take her to a hospital without technically arresting her, would it be OK to warn the "customer" and not arrest him? Yes, it would be ethical to do so.

Write a report detailing your actions. Why complicate matters in the report by mentioning the "customer" when you did not arrest him? Because it's the right thing to do. If you have taken the time to be a skilled student of law, you will know that a police officer has the power to take this course of action. It has to do with whether the officer, as an agent of the government, has anything to gain. Decisions not to arrest and to take a person to the hospital for treatment are rarely found to have been wrong. Decisions to arrest and not give medical treatment are much more likely to be problematic. We're back to the fundamental question: What action would you want a police officer to take if this person were your mother, father, or another person close to you?

5.   Whether to give the order to kill

You are the commander of a SWAT team. An adult male, the father of a five-month-old infant, has a domestic dispute with his wife. He hits her. She leaves their apartment and calls the police. The husband barricades himself in the apartment, saying that if anyone enters he will kill the baby. Some time later, during negotiations, he walks out of the apartment with a knife near the crying baby's chin, saying he will slit its throat if the police move. He is coming down the sidewalk with the baby in his arms. Your lead sniper radios you that he "can take the man out" with one shot. He asks if he has the "green light" to kill the man. It's your call.

What would you do?

Discussion

Negative! He does not have the green light! The only time a police officer should use deadly physical force is when all other means of handling the situation have been tried and have failed. It is used as an absolute last resort to protect the life of an officer or a third person.

6. Whether to enable and/or allow corruption

You are a narcotics detective in the process of serving a search warrant for crack cocaine in a filthy apartment infested with roaches. It's you, your partner (who is your lifelong friend), six other detectives, and a supervisor. You and your partner are told to search the bedroom. You see your partner find a money clip containing a large fold of bills and put it in his jeans pocket. It's obvious he doesn't know you saw him, and he doesn't turn the money in to the evidence officer. You ask him to step into the apartment's bathroom, close the door, and ask him about the money. At first he denies having found any money, but then he says, "It's only drug money. I would never take anything from a real person. I'll split it with you."

What would you do?

Discussion

I know what you're thinking. Take the money from him and turn it in to the evidence officer, reporting that you found it in the bedroom under the mattress. Or, threaten your partner with reporting the matter to your supervisor if he doesn't turn in the money. At first glance, both courses of action have elements of "rightness" attached to them. Once the money is turned in, you can then take on the task of getting your partner the help he obviously needs. It's an honorable way of dealing with the situation. After all, it *is* drug money. It isn't as if he stole the money from an innocent victim.

Actually, he has stolen the money from an innocent victim, but the victim isn't the issue here. The issue is that your partner committed a crime. It's not just your partner's integrity that's on the line here: it's the integrity of *all* police officers *everywhere*. There are only two viable choices. Arrest him, and report the matter to the supervisor at the scene, or report the matter to the supervisor at the scene and assist in arresting him. Will it be difficult to do? Yes. Will this decision impact the rest of your career? Yes. Will you be ostracized by many officers in the department for turning in your partner? Yes. After doing the right thing, do you then abandon your friend and go your own way? No. His behavior and comments may be indicative of psychological impairment, posttraumatic stress syndrome, or a host of other variables that may have affected his judgment. After the arrest, a friend would do everything possible to help him. This may take a lifetime. Although it may seem like the arrest was the difficult ethical decision, in reality the helping part after the arrest may prove to be the true test of your ethics and character.

7.   Whether to accept gratuities

A.   You are on duty and eat a meal at a restaurant on your beat or in your sector, and when you ask the waiter for the bill, the manager comes to your table and says, "It's on the house, officer. We just appreciate your coming in here to eat."

What would you do?

B.   You are off duty and eat a meal at a restaurant on your beat or in your sector, and when you ask the waiter for the bill, the manager comes to your table and says, "You look very familiar to me. Are you a police officer?" You answer that you are. The manager smiles broadly, shrugs his shoulders, and says, "You know we don't charge cops in here. Why do you embarrass me by asking for a bill?"

What would you do?

C.   You pull your cruiser up to the window of a fast-food joint after ordering a coffee to go. The window opens, you're handed a coffee, and the window closes. You honk the cruiser's horn and hold up a dollar bill. The cashier waves at you and disappears from the window.

What would you do?

D. You enter a flower shop, in uniform, to buy some flowers to take home to your spouse. You select a dozen roses. When presented with the bill, you notice "50% discount—Police" is written down at the bottom.

What would you do?

E. You're called in from the street by the desk lieutenant who gives you a large food order written on a piece of paper and instructs you to go to a specific restaurant. When you ask for the money to pay for the food, the lieutenant instructs you to tell the restaurant manager that the food is for "the boys in blue."

What would you do?

Discussion

A. There are no circumstances in which police officers should accept gratuities—or even be *perceived* as accepting a gratuity. Thank the manager for his gesture, tell him you think police officers should be treated like any other customer, ask for the bill, and pay it in full. If he refuses to give you a bill, leave slightly more money than you think is on the bill, and do not eat there in the future.

B. It's not wrong to have a meal in a restaurant on your beat or in your sector when you're off duty. However, if you suspected the restaurant "caters" to police officers, then it was poor judgment to enter that establishment. The ethical response to the manager remains the same as above. Tell the manager you think police officers should be treated just like any other customer. Ask for the bill, and pay it in full. Do not return.

C.   Enter the establishment and pay for the coffee.

D.   It is not using good judgment to engage in this type of personal activity while working. What about during the lunch hour? Police officers have a different responsibility from other workers. Remember, policing is a way of life, not a job. People who see an officer shopping don't know it's his or her lunch hour, so it's the wrong thing to do. Any type or amount of police discount is a gratuity, a form of graft, and unethical. Tell whomever presented you the bill that you think police officers should be treated like any other customer. Insist the bill be corrected, and pay the full price. Do not return.

E.   Tell the lieutenant that unless you receive money to pay for the food you will not go. If the lieutenant is foolish enough to give you a direct order to go get the food, and you were convinced it would be a gratuity, it would be unethical to obey the order. Such an order is improper and not legal. A high-ranking supervisor is directing a subordinate to commit an act which may be criminal.

8.   Whether to enforce the law equally

Complaints have been received about non-permitted cars parked in handicapped spaces at a hospital. You have been directed by your supervisor to ticket such cars. Upon arriving at the hospital parking lot, you see three cars without permits and one car with a permit parked in handicapped spaces. You put tickets on two of the non-permitted cars.

As you're placing a ticket on the third car, an elderly woman on crutches comes out of the hospital and says, "I'm sorry, officer. I've had a handicapped parking permit for years, but I've misplaced it."

One of the drivers of the other cars you ticketed approaches during the conversation between you and the elderly woman and says, "Hey, if you take back her ticket, you'd better take back mine!"

What would you do?

Discussion

We could have a long discussion here about verifying the elderly woman's statement by calling the state motor vehicle department, checking computerized records through the police communications division, and so on. All entail having an elderly woman on crutches wait around because a police officer doubts her word. Once again, if this was your mother or grandmother, what would you want the police officer to do? Whether or not she has a valid permit, she is obviously handicapped and needed to park close to the hospital. What is to be gained by issuing her a ticket? Deterrence? Take back the ticket, explain what could have happened, and urge her to replace her permit. Assist her in getting into the car. If required by department regulations, write a report as to why you took back the ticket.

What do you do with the man who demanded that his ticket also be canceled? His ticket stands. Explain to him the procedure used in your city or town to object to parking tickets. He has a right to take whatever legal action he feels is necessary.

9. Whether to intervene or remain silent

You and your partner have arrested a man for sexually assaulting a five-year-old child. The man was caught in the act, and the child is on the way to the hospital with serious injuries. The man resisted arrest, and it took four police officers to put him in handcuffs and get him into the police cruiser. During the arrest, he bit your partner's leg, breaking the skin, but not so bad as to require stitches. While transporting the prisoner to headquarters, the man continually spits at you from behind the cage in the rear seat and beats his head against the cruiser's windows. It's late at night, and your partner suddenly detours around a vacant building and says, "It's time to do some retraining and give this guy a little taste of street justice." Your partner gets out of the cruiser, takes out his blackjack, and drags the prisoner out of the back seat by his hair. He begins hitting him with the blackjack.

What would you do? (By the way, your partner is your closest friend. He was the best man at your wedding and is godfather of your son. His wife and yours are as close as sisters.)

Discussion

Once taken into police custody, the prisoner is in your care, and you are personally responsible for his safety. It is not enough to stop your partner from beating the prisoner and then getting the prisoner medical treatment. Your closest friend, the best man at your wedding and the godfather of your son, committed a crime. He must be placed under arrest, and a full report of what occurred must be brought to the attention of your supervisor. The real ethical dilemma comes afterward and is similar to that in situation 6. Will you stand by your friend after turning him in, when he no longer considers you a friend, but an enemy? How strong will your ethics be when his family, and maybe even your own family, turns against you? Will your character give you strength when the prisoner later claims you also beat him? The true test of ethics comes when the decisions are not easy and everyone around you says it would have been better had you done nothing. This is what separates the *warrior* from everyone else.

10. Whether to be a cop or a civilian

Your nephew is getting married, and you have been invited to his stag party, which is going to take place in another city. You have made it clear that you will attend so long as there are no violations of the law, meaning no topless women, no illegal gaming, and no underage drinking. You're told that everyone understands what you do for a living and that there will be "no problem." Shortly after everyone at the stag finishes eating, the music starts playing, and three scantily clad women enter the room and begin dancing for the groom. Soon, their tops are off, and they are lap dancing.

What would you do?

Discussion

Leave. There are many social occasions during which situations arise that pose ethical dilemmas for police officers. These range from someone casually lighting up a marijuana cigarette or doing a line of cocaine in front of an officer to admitting in conversation that they have committed a violent crime. As we have discussed, what will be the right thing to do may be different from what is required by law or department regulations.

Don't put yourself in a position where you are associating with people you know to be prone to this type of behavior. If it does occur, remember that you are a police officer twenty-four hours a day. If it would be appropriate for you to arrest a person if you were working, then it is just as appropriate to do so when you are off duty. If you're outside of your jurisdiction, use common sense in deciding whether the matter should be reported to the local police.

During my career, I was faced with these types of ethical dilemmas many times, and if you have been a police officer for any length of time, you probably have been too. Although several of the cases, such as "To kill or not to kill," present situations at the far end of the decision-making spectrum, all of the ethical considerations are quite common in policing. We could spend hours debating the finer points of each and every one of these ethical dilemmas, and by adding or subtracting subtle elements from each, come up with different ways of handling the situations. However, regardless of which "component of rightness" we are debating, ethics are about being able to determine what is right and doing it in the face of pressures from both within and without. One of the reasons it's so difficult to discipline ourselves to recognize that our decisions involve ethical choices is that we have a tendency to leave our ethics at home when we go to work. However, there are no separate private and public ethics. That's why ethical behavior is so unfashionable. It's a twenty-four-hours-a-day way of thinking. Taking the path of least resistance requires little effort and may reap momentary rewards; doing what is right requires a total expenditure of the self, and the rewards are timeless.

CHAPTER 2

Shepherding the Flock

*If a man does not keep pace with his companions, perhaps it is
because he hears a different drummer. Let him step to the music
which he hears, however measured or far away.*

Henry David Thoreau

☯ CONFLICTING VALUES AND ETHICS: IS OUR TRIBE IN TROUBLE?

During the past several years I've had the opportunity to travel across the United States and meet with police officers from all levels of the criminal justice system: state troopers, agents of the FBI and DEA, sheriffs, rangers, big city street cops, and small town police officers. I'm convinced that our unbroken tradition of courage in the face of danger and stepping in harm's way to protect other people is alive and well. The brave, courageous, and bold continue to patrol our streets and are ready to lay down their lives in the service of their country. However, a significant number of officers I've spoken with have fallen away from the path and no longer hear the pounding of the drums. Although their actions may be legally acceptable, they ignore the need to identify and resolve the moral issues involved. Hearing conflicting answers to ethical questions, they seem to lack the inner strength necessary to sift through alternative courses of action when moral issues are involved. Constant exposure to the stressful nature of policing and "living between worlds" has caused them to turn down the light of awareness and drown out the voice of reason. The defense mechanisms and psychological hardness that many officers build around themselves to deaden the pain of what they see and are required to do hardens their hearts and distorts their judgment.

I recently was invited to a police conference in Atlantic City, New Jersey, attended by police officers from the United States and Europe.

I had the opportunity to meet with officers singly and in groups of two or three. When I asked them how they liked policing, most responded with "it's just a job" and seemed amused when I encouraged them to embrace policing as a "way of life." Instead, they spoke about looking forward to their retirement, even though most of them had been on the job only a few years. At seminars, training sessions, and trade shows, all the officers I meet say they want to do the right thing, but many seem baffled as to what the "right" thing is. It's not that they have the will to do wrong, just a marked indifference to doing what is right! Others are lost in the jungle of the streets and have reverted to being little more than mercenaries. Some are unhappy with their "jobs" and life in general, so they just go through the motions and try to stay out of the system's way; they speak of policing in terms of "surviving" the system. Still others describe a feeling of "emptiness" in their lives, having taken the oath but not embracing the code that goes along with it. They don't seem to understand that with great power comes an even greater responsibility to exercise moral reasoning to resolve ethical dilemmas.

Complaints about the criminal justice system, plea bargains, working conditions, contractual "give-backs," and lack of command leadership are fairly common in policing. Griping is an art form in law enforcement. Yet from an ethical standpoint, many officers who do seek the "right way," are carried along by the tide and look in the wrong places. They look for the approval of their peers instead of examining their own consciences and acting on the strength of their convictions. Because separating oneself from the group is so difficult to do in policing, it's much easier for a police officer to join his or her peers in what I call "anti-awfulizing." "Anti-awfulizing" is the offloading of individual responsibility by police officers for their failure to do the things necessary to have a positive impact on the people they serve. This is accomplished by blaming the city or town administrators, the courts, the chief of police, the department's higher-ranking officers, and even their own union for not allowing them to do their jobs. This not only creates a negative work environment, it also contributes to officers becoming paralyzed by stagnation, indifference, frustration, and apathy.

Many in our tribe are in trouble and are living lives of quiet desperation. As one police officer laughingly put it, "We just do feel-good policing. If it feels good, we do it. If we don't feel like it, we don't do it." In other words, their ethical system is based on narcissism, self-gratification, and situational ethics. They have lost the ability to distinguish between self-regarding behavior and the kind of other-regarding behavior that is so crucial in the care-giving professions.

I'm often bewildered and saddened when I hear comments such as these from police officers. In contrast, I remember being disappointed when my shift was about to end, and it was time to go home. I and the cops I served with were having such a good time catching crooks, we wanted to stay and do more of it! In fact, the last time I broke a couple of fingers and my hand was in a splint, I tried to hide in the back line at roll call so the sergeant wouldn't find out and send me home. I wasn't any different from the other officers; we all felt this way. It was the way we were trained, taught, guided, and led. Our level of expectation for each other's behavior was exceptionally high, but we didn't realize it because our esprit de corps was so interwoven with our perception of who we were. I was proud of the officers I worked with and proud to tell people I was a Hartford police officer!

So I don't use terms like "new centurions" to describe this breed of police officer. I call them "shooting stars." A shooting star is a person walking the path of a *warrior* who has become burned out and has lost "the way." This type of police officer is easily drawn off of the path by false promises of money, status, power, and the adulation of others. Because they haven't disciplined themselves, they have no control over their lives, and they become passive spectators to events unfolding around them. They give in to anxiety because they don't know what principles of action to believe in. Seeing no positive effects of their work over long periods of time, they distance themselves by offering poor and impersonal service. Some shooting stars become "comets," which is an almost-*warrior* who has become shackled by fear of failing, or sometimes of succeeding, and has gone berserk. Many of our brothers and sisters are self-medicating on coke, crack, alcohol, heroin, and barbiturates. Research compiled by Michael Posner and reported in the *Boston Globe* indicates that more than twice as many police officers committed suicide in 1994—three hundred—than were killed in the line of duty by guns or any other means (Posner 1994). Wearing the bag, the police uniform, can be a killer if you don't frequently take the time to step back and personally examine the ethical framework forming the foundation of your character. Ethical behavior requires continual self-reflection and a weighing of choices. Those without a strong sense of self-worth fall prey to making decisions based on the will of the group or the fad of the moment without sensing the long-term consequences to themselves and others.

❺ VALUES AND ETHICS: THE CORNERSTONES OF THE PATH OF THE WARRIOR

Unfortunately, examples of breakdowns in police ethics are not difficult to find. The Rodney King case and the riots in Los Angeles following the acquittal in April 1992 of four white police officers who had been videotaped beating him, the actions and testimony of police officers in the O.J. Simpson case, and the videotaping of police officers beating illegal immigrants after a prolonged chase of their vehicle are recent sobering examples. Who can forget the testimony in the Simpson case of the renown forensic expert Dr. Henry Lee when he remarked, "Something wrong here!"

As recently as September of 1996, the Associated Press reported that in August, sixteen drunken members of an "elite" Indianapolis police unit "stumbled out of a downtown bar grabbing their crotches and making lewd remarks to women before beating up a black man who confronted them." The chief of police resigned over the incident, prompting mayor Stephen Goldman to remark, "No one knows what happened that night. It's clear some police officers acted inappropriately, it's also clear some did nothing wrong" (Jewell 1996). As Dr. Lee would say, "Something wrong here!"

These examples provide glimpses into the secretive inner world of policing, due primarily to advances in communication technology, such as videotaping, which allow the public to see firsthand the behavior and conduct of some of its police officers. Obviously, we wish the media would exert as much effort in reporting the outstanding, often heroic, work done by officers throughout the country every day. However, the fact that it's not our success stories but the improper behavior of police officers that makes front page news points out the high standards our society expects from the men and women who serve and protect them. As pointed out by Air Force

General and Chief of Staff Ronald R. Fogleman in a recent message to military officers, "We defend our nation. The tools of our trade are lethal. We are held to a higher standard by the public, and we are held in high regard by the public because of the integrity we demonstrate by holding ourselves accountable and others accountable for their action." Perhaps we should place the general's words on huge signs in the front lobby of our police stations.

So what is it that our police officers *should do* when faced with the types of ethical dilemmas described in this book? Simply put, *warriors* choose to walk a separate path, different from others. They take the risk of standing alone and of speaking up when others are silent. A vital component of ethical behavior is feeling obligated to do what is right. To feel obligated, one must not only care but be willing to pay the hard price that comes in wrestling with one's own conscience. *Warriors* are self-actuated. They project consequences into the future and think, plan, and live long range. *Warriors* take personal control over their lives rather than be passive spectators and the victims of events occurring around them.

All *warriors* are "works in progress." As Aristotle reasoned, we become moral by practicing moral acts. He wrote, "We become just by doing just acts, temperate by doing temperate acts, and brave by doing brave acts." In commenting on Aristotle's statement that "an ethical decision is one that is made by an ethical person," Martin B. Copenhauver said, "Only when character, rather than choice, becomes central to ethics can we make sense out of Aristotle's statement" (Copenhauver 1994).

Although true *warriors* are difficult to find, many people want to become *warriors* and begin walking the path, but they allow their energy to be taken from them and their light to dim. You can see it in their eyes. They want the rewards, but they are no longer willing to pay the price to fill the lamp with the kind of oil that keeps it from growing dim. They have lowered their self-esteem and feel a constant need to prove themselves to others.

⑤ ACTIVATING YOUR BELIEF SYSTEM

Your ethics—your belief system composed of values, attitudes, and moral principles in action—are the cornerstone on which strong character is built. Basic beliefs and values act as guides that yield our identity, establish inner and outer boundaries, and create expectations of the way we should behave. Firm convictions about how we should behave shape our conduct and help to identify the personal goals we feel are valuable to achieve. Continuous practice of positive habits leads to "virtue"—the quality of recognizing and doing the right thing. All are a direct consequence of internally generated practices. Values help define who we are and the meaning we attach to our lives, and they shape our thinking. Our personal convictions serve as the ground rules for determining our ethical decisions. It's often our individual attitudes and belief systems that are in need of attention. Attitudes are learned and have a major impact on our behavior. Human behavior often is a matter of custom or habit and little thought is given to why or how we are behaving in a certain manner. Since our attitudes change over time and are evaluative in nature, it is through the use of reason coupled with ethics that convictions previously held may be altered. Favorable or unfavorable attitudes toward other people, issues, and events reflect basic feelings, individual preferences, and values. Attitudes are the cords that bind and shape behavior.

When we choose to do what we know is wrong, when we devalue ourselves and our personal dignity, an unbalancing of our value system occurs. We call this unbalancing our "conscience." Because our attitudes and belief system are uniquely our own, we have the power to change them. But without following the path that is right for us, without improving the "quality" of our thoughts through the continuous training and disciplining of the mind toward individual happiness, the days blur together, flowing into a ritualized pattern that we blindly follow. Our conception of who we are and what we want is lost, and we no longer view our lives as having significance. Because of what we see and are required to do as law enforcement officers, our immediate emotional responses sometimes overwhelm our ability to effectively reason. That is one of the reasons why self-discipline is so vital to those who wear the badge and carry the gun.

☯ THE EFFECTS OF LOWER ENTRY-LEVEL STANDARDS ON POLICE ETHICS

One of the ethical issues currently being debated in the law enforcement community is whether entry-level standards and police testing are producing the kind of candidate who has the psychological hardiness and intrinsic morality requisite to a successful career in policing. All law enforcement officers face the test of the sands of time. The creed we learned in the police academy is often quickly unlearned the moment officers hit the street and attempt to apply it to real life. Even with a probationary period spent working with another officer in coach-pupil fashion, the transition from the police academy to the reality of the streets is abrupt. To avoid criticism and gain acceptance, new officers must learn to conform to the standards set by the more experienced officers (Braswell 1992). Many officers lack the inner qualities necessary to deal with being "the man," having the power that goes along with the badge and the gun. In a study of police personality published in *Behind the Shield,* Arthur Niederhoffer found that nearly eighty percent of first-day recruits believed that the police department was an "efficient, smoothly operating organization." However, two months later, less than a third professed that belief. Similarly, half the recruits believed that a police supervisor is "very interested in the welfare of his subordinates," yet two months later that number declined to thirteen percent" (Neiderhoffer 1967). There is little doubt that new police officers are quickly socialized toward a cynical view of people and events occurring around them. The ambivalent attitude of the public, the social isolation that comes with the job, and the dangers faced in enforcing the law all combine to create an esprit de corps more accurately described as "you're either with us or against us." Although this is not completely negative, it's important to recognize how difficult it is for a police officer to break away from the tribal nature of policing and make ethical decisions based on individual reasoning as opposed to the will of the group.

Since a person's ethics and character are difficult to test for in an economical manner that will also withstand court challenges, many of the methods once used to determine the "character" of a person desiring to be a police officer have been eliminated. In many of our cities and towns, you can now wear a badge and carry a gun even if you have admitted to having used illicit drugs, such as marijuana or cocaine, as long as you didn't garner a profit by selling it to others. Consider the following excerpt from a medium-sized police department's "Guidelines for Acceptance of Police Officer Candidates" and its implications for ethical conduct by police officers.

Applicants should not be rejected for experimental use of cocaine not to exceed three separate occurrences which shall not have occurred within the past eighteen months.

It is difficult for me to understand why a community would allow a person who is an admitted illegal drug user to become a police officer. Yet, even criminal convictions no longer prohibit people from entry into law enforcement, so long as the person didn't commit too bad a crime and it didn't happen recently. Consider the fact that one recent survey found that about twenty-two percent of the 67,000 applicants for police jobs are rejected because they were "deceptive" on the polygraph screening in their background investigation (Horvath 1993).

Physical fitness tests are slowly being eliminated. Courts have ruled that they have not been proven to be job related. The latest catch phrases are that the police should reflect the community they serve, and we should celebrate diversity. Translated, this means we should be recruiting more ethnic minorities and women into policing. I agree, but we should still be striving for people who are not "average" citizens of the community. We should be recruiting individuals who possess the potential to be role models for all of us to look up to. No police officer I ever admired was either average or a reflection of the community. They all marched to the beat of a different drummer. Our goal should be to attract people into law enforcement who not only have the knowledge, skills, and abilities to do the job, but also have the ethics, personal traits, and psychological hardiness society expects from those entrusted to serve and protect them.

☯ THE DOWNWARD CYCLE

We have long known that a police officer's job is so stressful and demanding that even a saint would have difficulty reasoning through the types of ethical dilemmas police officers face every day. So we need to find ways to interrupt the cycle of idealism, reality, apathy, and burnout that has become so prevalent among people trying to walk the path of a *warrior* today. It's not just cops who sink through these stages—it's social workers, priests, nurses, doctors, lawyers, corrections officers, probation officers, and all who serve others in a "helping" profession. Acknowledging that this cycle is problematic in policing helps push the development of intervention techniques that can mitigate its negative effects. Following is a description of the various phases of the cycle so you'll have a better understanding of how they affect the ethical decision-making process of police officers and other care givers. See if the descriptions remind you of anyone you know.

☯ Idealism

Idealism is a state of mind in which you truly believe you can make a significant difference in people's lives. A young man or woman dreams of becoming a police officer, a member of the thin blue line. Whether they caught the fever from reruns of *NYPD Blue,* a movie about cops, a member of their family, or a police-officer friend doesn't really matter. They heard the pounding of the drums and answered the call to adventure.

It's very difficult to be hired as a police officer today. Those who make it through the civilian testing process (thousands may apply for a handful of positions) and the police academy (only about eighty percent do), hit the streets with the feeling that they were chosen by a higher power to solve all of society's problems. Most people become police officers because they want to help people, and it can be a source of inner conflict when their expectations are tested by the reality of the streets.

☯ Reality

Unfortunately for most, the second stage—reality—confronts them relatively quickly. Rookie police officers find they are just a cog in a very big wheel. The sociological and socioeconomic problems of society are so overwhelming—gang violence, riots, homelessness, drugs, whole sections of cities a virtual no-man's land, housing projects full of crack houses—of course it's almost impossible for one person to solve them. For those with a little inner fortitude and a few amulets and shields, the process of moving from idealism to reality may take several years. It's between idealism and reality where many become disappointed and begin to lose their shadow, or the certainty that their lives have significance.

☯ Apathy

Somewhere between the stages of reality and burnout, apathy sets in—the "feel-good policing" described earlier: just coming to work, staying out of everyone's way, and going home. When there are too many calls for police services and too many people to help, it's easier to develop a brusque, impersonal method for dealing with them. Not being able to help everyone is so anguishing for care givers that in order not to feel it, they build a wall between themselves and those who are in need of service. Over time, this mentally callous and inhumane way of dealing with people is manifested in callous and dehumanized behaviors. People are then treated as objects to be dealt with rather than fellow human beings. Burnout usually follows this stage.

☯ Burnout

So, that enthusiastic young person who came on the job at twenty-one is a shell of his or her former self at thirty-five. Married, divorced; maybe twice. Self-medicates a lot in order to escape the emotional pain. Alcohol, barbiturates, and sometimes the harder drugs. Spends a lot of time alone because, after all, the only people who understand him or her are other cops and sometimes nurses. Short fuse at work, but it takes a bomb to go off before he or she acts interested in anything outside of work. Sound familiar?

If we want our police officers to have such qualities as prudence, faith, hope, charity, humility, and fortitude and to strive for justice tempered with mercy, then we must recognize that the job itself requires extraordinary people who can withstand the psychological and physical effects of doing it. There is no more important function in a democracy than the choosing of who will be allowed to enforce our laws and regulate our conduct.

☯ SOME THOUGHTS ABOUT HAVING LOST YOUR SHADOW

One way to think about a loss of enthusiasm for police work, the feeling that something is missing from life, is by using the image of a shadow to represent something that has been lost but under the right circumstances can be found again. You may have lost your shadow without even knowing it. Explaining what your shadow is, when you lost it, and why it's important to find it again, is one of the central themes of this book. Oh, there's probably nothing dramatically wrong with your life, it's just that *you* know what your potential is, what you could be, and what you could accomplish, if only things were different. Every day we meet people who have dried up like a raisin, deferring their dreams to some distant future. Occasionally we pause and catch a fleeting glimpse of something important that is missing, but we rationalize that we will be happy when we finally reach the goals that often others have set for us. Some people achieve a great deal but lack the ability to enjoy it. So we tone down our awareness and sleepwalk through our busy existence. By the time we finally awaken to discover that our lives lack meaning, the web we have woven for ourselves is too strong to break. The pattern of our lives has become so rote that we are afraid to make the changes required to break free.

Our dreams become reality only through action. There is a genie of great power residing within you, and it's time to stop waiting for things to get better and do something about it. It is only through the continuous force of the will that we exercise power over ourselves and accept responsibility for our own happiness. You have begun the journey to take positive control of your life by hearing the pounding of the drums and answering the call to explore new frontiers. It's never too late to begin practicing the ancient skills and walking the path of a *warrior*. As an old Turkish proverb advises, "No matter how far you have gone on a wrong road, turn back." You *want* what all human beings crave in their inner hearts. You want to be worthy of praise, to accomplish something that has lasting value, and to feel good about yourself. To affirm your own self integrity. You want to be happy, to live in harmony with yourself and others. To love and be loved. To return to a time when everything that could be dreamed was still possible. When you would bound out of bed in the morning excited to begin a new day rather than dreading it. A time when there were no difficult decisions to be made because everything was possible. A time when you still had your shadow. All of this and more is possible if you unlock the gate and begin walking the path of a *warrior*. I am your seneschal, the gatekeeper, and I will show you the paths that lead to the way and provide the map that will help you find your shadow again.

War Story

I recently had dinner with Johnny the "Chin" Evans. He has a cleft in his chin like Kirk Douglas, so naturally he was dubbed "Chin" early on in his career. Johnny was commander of the vice and narcotics squad in a major northeastern city where I had given a lecture. We were discussing Robert Bly (1992) and Joseph Campbell's (1990) concept of the shadow and my adaptation of parts of it to posttraumatic stress syndrome. I was surprised when Johnny told me the story of how he discovered his shadow was missing and how he thought something about the way he was living his life might be wrong.

Johnny is one of those guys that looks like a freight train. He's a smaller version of Paul Bunyan with big tufts of hair growing out of his ears and hands the size of horseshoes. He even has muscles on the back of his scalp. They wrinkle up and down when he moves. So I was surprised that Johnny opened up to me so quickly because it usually takes quite a bit of time for officers. He had been without his shadow for a long time, but like a lot of us, he didn't recognize that something wasn't quite right.

It happened about two weeks before we had dinner, on Christmas Eve, in the middle of a narcotics raid in one of the city's housing projects. He and his men had been serving search warrants all week, sometimes three or four a day. All were forcible entry. You know how it works. A bunch of unmarked police cruisers speed down a street, car doors fly open, and everyone jumps out all at once. You run up a couple flights of concrete stairs until you get to the right door.

"Police! Search warrant!"

No one ever answers, and the process of battering down the steel door with a ram or sledge hammer begins. Johnny said that this door popped quickly, the shotgun man made his sweep, and all of them got in safely. The only people inside were a young mother and her three children.

Johnny's people had gotten a search warrant the day before hitting the place, but to be on the safe side, they had sent a snitch up to buy a couple hours before they went in. The snitch had told them there were hundreds of vials of crack in the house and the guy they were after, "Big Henry" Thompson, was there. He wasn't.

The woman told them "Big Henry" had just left to get some milk for the kids. Johnny and his guys searched all the usual places, but they didn't find so much as a glassine bag. So, they began searching the usual unusual places, such as the inside of the television set and the ice cube trays. The woman and her three children were huddled in one corner of the living room near the Christmas tree. It was the only place they hadn't thoroughly searched. It had begun to snow, and Johnny was looking out the window wondering if he would get home in time to celebrate Christmas Eve with his wife and children.

One of his guys came over to him and said, "Lieu, we're coming up dry. Do you want us to search the presents?" The narc motioned with his head over to the Christmas tree where a bunch of neatly wrapped presents surrounded its base. "It's the only place we haven't looked."

Johnny looked over at the seven or eight guys with him and said, "Yeah, open them up," and a couple of his men began unwrapping the presents. Johnny said the woman began howling in his general direction, and he told her to take the kids into the other room. One of the little girls—he described her as being about five years old with long pigtails and the largest brown eyes he had ever seen—began sobbing.

He walked over and reached out his arms to hug her, but she cried, "No, no, no, stay away from me!"

She was trembling with fear and tears were streaming down her face. She was terrified. Johnny said that it was when he looked into those big brown terrified eyes that he realized he had lost his shadow. He told me that he remembers thinking it wasn't supposed to be like this. Children were supposed to run to him for protection, not run away scared of him. Johnny the "Chin," giant of a man that he was, had such a heavy heart he couldn't stay in the apartment any longer. He ran down the stairs and ended up walking along the street in the snowstorm until one of his men came after him and convinced him to get in the cruiser. Johnny said he had left the apartment because he didn't want his men to see him crying. The fact that his guys found three hundred vials of crack in one of the Christmas presents didn't make him feel any better. For some reason it made him feel worse.

On his long ride home that night, Johnny reflected on what had happened and realized that he had lost his passion for the job. No more fire in the belly. He didn't want to do this anymore. He and his men were running up and down stairs all over the city to find the residue of some plant, be it marijuana, heroin, or coke. They seized drugs, money, and guns but weren't even making a dent. Johnny said he remembers thinking, "This isn't police work; it's a medical and psychological problem."

I reminded Johnny that he was only doing his job and that questioning what we do and how we do it is a pretty good indication that we're OK. I also reminded him that what he did for a living was honorable, that few people had his skills, and he was fortunate to be around people who cared about him. However, the wound was still too fresh and no amount of talk over dinner could shake Johnny's conviction that he had reached a crossroads in his life. Indeed he had. His values and belief systems were conflicting with what he was doing at work and shaking the foundation of who he was.

About a month after we broke bread together, I finally convinced Johnny the "Chin" to attend a retreat with me. Cops are socialized from day one to hide their emotions and work out their problems on their own. Of course, there is also the stigma against showing any sort of weakness. It took a call to Johnny's wife to finally get him to come with me. I chose a monastery where I've gone before to re-energize. Cops are resilient. Johnny had worked through most of what he perceived to be his problem, and my job was merely to be a good listener, provide him with a few shields to use in the future, and allow him to use some of my energy. Johnny had become a functional alcoholic and my role was to convince him that he needed to enroll in a treatment program before he ended up like so many of our brothers and sisters who have turned to the dark side.

A few weeks ago, I received a call from Johnny the "Chin" inviting me to spend a couple of days with him.

When I gave the address the "Chin" had given me to the cabby at the airport, he turned around in the seat and said, "Are you sure this is where you want to go?"

"Yeah, I'm sure. Why?" I replied.

"It's not the best neighborhood," he mumbled.

The cabby was right. When we finally pulled up to the address, at first all I could see was what looked like abandoned buildings.

"Which one?" I asked the cabby.

He pointed with his cigar to a large brick building across the street. As I walked toward it, I made out a small sign over the front door that read "Police Athletic League." When I opened the door, all of my senses were assaulted with noise. There were cops and kids everywhere. A basketball game was going full tilt in the middle of a makeshift court, some kids were lifting weights in one corner, and a karate class was going on in another. Several boom boxes were blasting, kids were pounding the heavy bag, and two young men were boxing in a ring with a referee. The stands were filled with parents and kids who were waiting their turn to get in on the action.

In the middle of all of this was Johnny the "Chin." He was wearing an oversized sweatshirt emblazoned with "Coach" and a pair of multicolored Hawaiian shorts. A whistle hung from a chain around his big neck. Johnny had just called the basketball out of bounds on one of the teams and was in the middle of arguing with the players when he saw me. He gave me a wide grin, trotted over, and playfully slapped me on the shoulder. I pretended it didn't hurt.

"So, what do you think?" he asked, twirling around with outstretched arms to take in the entire complex.

I was completely speechless, and this seemed to please him immensely. Over lunch, the "Chin" proudly told me that he was the new commander of the police academy. The police athletic league fell under the academy's authority, and he tried to spend one day a week there. Johnny proceeded to give me a rapid-fire lecture on how important it is to train new police officers the "right way," how he is a born teacher and had missed his calling, and how this gave him an opportunity to "give back" to new officers what many veteran police officers had taught him over the years. Johnny was happy. He had found his shadow again, the certainty that his life is significant.

I asked the "Chin" what had happened to turn his life back around. I guess I secretly hoped it was something I might have said to him on the retreat.

He seemed to sense this and said, "Well, the retreat helped. I gave a lot of thought to what you said about no one else being responsible for my happiness and all that bullshit. But, it was making the plan that really helped me. I was able to sit down and take a hard look at my life, and figure out what I wanted to do and how to do it. My wife helped me. She attends AA meetings with me, and I know I'm not out of the woods yet, but I haven't had a drink in months.

"I walked into the chief's office and told him I wanted to teach or I was going to retire. I was so surprised when he put me in charge of the academy."

We left the restaurant and walked the block back to the police athletic league building. When we were almost there, Johnny and I saw a woman and a little girl coming toward us on the sidewalk.

She broke away from her mother, ran up to the "Chin," and gave him a hug around the legs saying, "Hi, Uncle Johnny."

When the woman joined us, the "Chin" said to her, "How's Big Henry?"

"OK," she replied.

I looked from the woman to the "Chin" to the little girl with pigtails and the largest brown eyes I had ever seen. "You're not going to tell me this is the family from Christmas Eve, are you?" I asked Johnny.

He grinned and said, "Yep."

Sometimes the good guys do finish first, I thought. Johnny the "Chin" had found his shadow again, and like Peter Pan, he had returned to the things that drew him to policing in the first place—making a significant difference in other people's lives.

CHAPTER 3

Searching for Ancient Skills

☯ MAGICAL THINKING

The shadow is the part of you that has faith that you are special, have been chosen, and are unlike any other human being. Shadow dancing is an ancient skill we all have but may have forgotten how to use. Shadow dancing is what once allowed you to believe there was a pot of gold at the end of the rainbow and you could find it; that your guardian angel might appear at any time by your bedside to bestow miraculous powers; that a walk in the woods might very well result in an encounter with fairies and elves who would guide you to a cave where pirates had hidden a treasure chest overflowing with precious gems and gold doubloons; when your kindness to a hag would transform her into a good witch who would grant you three wishes. Our shadow provided us the inner energy of knowing that if we used just the right formula, wished and prayed using the correct words, practiced long enough and tried hard enough, we could drink our fill from the cup of happiness.

Our grown-up shadow is a well of positive thinking, the realization that joy and peace of mind are a direct result of the quality of our thoughts. Our shadows know that it's not what happens to us that determines our happiness, but how we choose to interpret our own reality. Many of us lose our shadow because over many years we are socialized to think negatively rather than positively. It's very difficult to retrain the mind to loosen its self-imposed shackles and interpret what's happening around us differently. It requires self-discipline and constant self-awareness. Sailing on the ocean of our dreams requires a firm destination and a plan of action to reach the safe haven of inner peace. To achieve positive growth we must arise from the slumber created by the constant stimulus of the outer world and give ourselves permission to be our own hero. Positive growth can't be imposed on us by other people, it can only come from the furnace we create inside ourselves. It is the by-product of internally generated practices that are positive in nature.

The reason many who become care-givers lose their way is that they buy into defining success as achievement at work, personal beauty, money, and the possession of material things. They strive to "fit in" and conform rather than be outstanding. Yet those who do achieve society's definition of success are often unhappy and spend a great deal of time and energy searching for a magic potion or using artificial tranquilizers to alter their state of consciousness. Like brightly burning candles, they consume themselves in exploring the darkness of greed and power. They harden their hearts to those who don't fit their definition of achievement while they become rich in gold but poor in happiness.

We're often surprised and a little suspicious when we encounter a person who is happy and at peace with themselves and the world around them. The kind of person who radiates energy—an inner light—that overflows into and around the people they are with. You feel better having been with them and take some of the glow of their light away with you. It's not unusual to lose track of time when you're with people who glow with this inner light. For a short while, you become energized, see things more clearly, recognize what's important and what isn't, and are able to visualize possibilities not thought about in many years. You begin to remember when you had your shadow. Then the glow begins to diminish as long-established habits and ritualized patterns of thinking and behavior create a veil between you and the light, leaving no space for your shadow to gain substance. We forget again that lasting joy and inner peace have nothing to do with the opinions of others. Self-worth, by its very definition, comes from within ourselves.

☯ FOR THE SKEPTICS

I know you're skeptical about whether the mind can be trained to "think differently." So was I. The rational you is probably in conflict with the spiritual you. Your inner custodian is setting off all kinds of warning bells about the realities of life, the terrible things that happen to good people over which they have no control, and the complexities of living in today's society. Of course all of this is true. Life does involve pain, difficulty, and loss. Each of us has had plenty of opportunities to see how the sons and daughters of Adam treat one another. You and I will be provided more than ample opportunity to suffer. My question to you is why continuously practice suffering while you're waiting? There are care-givers who live and work under horribly traumatic circumstances yet have tremendous positive impact on others. They are at peace, happy, and are conduits of positive energy. They have a positive effect on everyone with whom they have contact. Do these people know something that the rest of us don't? The answer is a qualified yes; qualified because all of us once knew the path to inner peace, but we were socialized to think that other people or material things were responsible for our happiness. Abraham Lincoln put it this way: "I have found that most people are about as happy as they make up their minds to be."

I will be discussing how to take control of your destiny in the next chapter on personal and professional development, but I want to ask some questions here so you can begin thinking about several things that are important for those who have chosen policing as a way of life.

1. Do you view what you do as a police officer as enforcing the law or helping people?

2. Do you look forward to going to work as a police officer, or do you see it as something you have to do to make money to support yourself and/or your family?

3. Are you proud to be a police officer, or are you defensive when telling others what you do for a living?

4. Are you happy? Is life a wonderful adventure for you? Do you laugh frequently and find joy in being with others? Have you realized yet that the only person responsible for your happiness is you?

⑨ SINS FROM THE PAST: CORRUPTION, POLITICS, AND CRIME

War Story

One of the first ethical dilemmas I faced during my career in law enforcement came shortly after graduation from the police academy. Back then we didn't have today's systematic method of furthering a new officer's education by assigning him or her to a field training officer. Once you were sworn in, you learned by doing. One of my first assignments was with a veteran officer working the paddy wagon, a police vehicle assigned to pick up people officers arrested and transport them back to the police department's jail section. The paddy wagon looked like a large post office truck, except it was painted entirely black and the inside of the rear section was a giant jail cell with wooden benches along all four walls. Pieces of metal had been welded to the benches so prisoners could be handcuffed where they sat, and a padlock was used to secure the rear doors.

Every morning the wagon's first stop was a small park in the heart of the business district where "balkies" (alcoholics) passed out after a night of drinking. Today, we take them to the hospital, but back then it was still unlawful to be drunk and passed out in the park, and the police routinely arrested them and took them to jail. So we drove the paddy wagon over to the park, and I and the officer (Alex the "Giant" Johnson, who was permanently assigned to this duty) roused the balkies and put them in the back of the wagon.

I had never done this before. In fact I had never even made an arrest, so I wasn't sure what I was supposed to do. The "Giant" told me to search all of the drunks as I put them in the wagon, and if I found any money to give it to him. Most were broke, but a couple did have a few crumpled dollars that I dutifully handed over to him. We left that park and went to two more, and within an hour had about twelve balkies in the back of the wagon. By my count, I had handed over twenty-four dollars to Officer Johnson, all taken from the people we had arrested. In my naiveté, I figured this was standard procedure, and I had carefully written down who I had taken the money from and how much. I figured that when we got to the station house and processed the prisoners, Johnson would turn the money in, and I would be told to fill out some sort of form listing who the money belonged to.

When we got to the station, I was immediately sent by the booking room sergeant to get everyone coffee. By the time I got back, all the prisoners had been placed in one big holding cell. I asked the sergeant what he wanted me to do with the list, and he said "What list?"

When I handed it to him, he studied it for what seemed like a long time and then gave it back to me saying, "Take this up with Officer Johnson." I began to get the inkling that something wasn't quite right, but being a rookie, as soon as we got back in the paddy wagon, I held up the list and said to Johnson, "What do you want me to do with this?"

He took the piece of paper, crumpled it up in a ball, and threw it out the window.

"I took care of it. That's all you need to know," he grunted.

Johnson didn't talk to me for the rest of the shift, and the next day I was assigned to a beat in one of the housing projects. I told the officer I was pounding the beat with what had happened, and he laughed, shaking his head saying, "He pocketed the money."

I couldn't believe it! I thought there must be some other explanation. After all, that was a crime! A police officer wouldn't do that. I didn't know what to do about it.

The money and the fact that I had taken it from the balkies and given it to Johnson kept gnawing at me. The more I thought about it, the angrier I got. So I made an appointment with my police academy sergeant and went to his office and told him what happened. I thought I was going to get fired. The sergeant listened to me very gravely and advised me there was no proof Johnson had taken the money. My sergeant said the best thing to do was take the matter up with Officer Johnson. I left the office feeling depressed and confused. In the police academy, we had a class on the law enforcement code of ethics and the department's code of conduct. I took them both quite seriously but was confused as to what was the right thing to do. It now seemed pretty clear to me that there was a good chance I had uncovered a criminal in our midst. However, maybe I was wrong and there was a procedure Johnson had followed that I didn't know about. I made it a point to dig out the department order on "prisoner property," and it specifically said that all money taken from a prisoner was to be given to the booking sergeant, who would issue the prisoner a receipt for it.

With the order in hand, I waited for Officer Johnson at his locker. When he showed up I showed him the order and asked him what he had done with the twenty-four dollars. At first he laughed. Then he told me to go away. I didn't. Finally he grabbed me by the throat and pulled me toward him saying, "Don't make an issue out of this kid. It could get you hurt."

That did it. I couldn't breathe, and right or wrong, I started swinging. Nothing connected, and Johnson just held me at arm's length.

When he saw that I wasn't going to stop, he said, "You're a nut case," and turning me loose reached into his locker and peeled off twenty-four dollars from a stash of bills. He yanked off my police hat, stuffed the bills inside, and said, "Here. Do what you want with it."

I took the money and left. I wrote a detailed report, put the money in a little envelope, clipped the envelope to my report, and turned the report in to the front desk.

I never heard another word about it. I was never called in, spoken to, or asked about the report or the money. However, about two weeks later Officer Johnson suddenly "retired," and I learned there had been an ongoing investigation into Johnson and a few other officers weeks before I had turned in my report. I felt a little better knowing that.

This incident had a profound effect on me. For one thing, it made me realize that I was totally responsible for my actions as a police officer, regardless of whether a "veteran" officer, or even a supervisor, was telling me what to do or how to do it. My naiveté, along with a failure to thoroughly know the department's policies and procedures, had allowed Officer Johnson to use me to take money from other people. I vowed it would never happen again, and during my next twenty-one years on the force, I would rarely see this type of corruption. The vast majority of the officers I served with were honest, hard working, courageous, and honorable.

However, not everyone who wears a badge and carries a gun fits that description. Since the inception of modern American law enforcement in the early part of the nineteenth century, the profession has been wracked by corruption and unethical behavior. A review of our checkered past will help put a later discussion of the "Law Enforcement Code of Ethics" into perspective.

☯ Early Policing: 1834–1900

It wasn't until the 1790s that our nation had even six cities with a population of over eight thousand people (Day 1974). This, coupled with early America's agricultural way of life, contributed to the slow development of municipal policing. As our young country moved from this rural, agricultural society toward a more industrialized nation, the sheriff of colonial America was gradually replaced by constables, the town marshall, and vigilantes. As cities grew in size and population, the nineteenth century saw pervasive urban unrest and mob violence, leading to the formation of America's first real police departments: Philadelphia's in 1833, Boston's in 1838, New York's in 1844, Chicago's in 1851, and New Orleans and Cincinnati's in 1852.

Police officers of that era were generally incompetent, corrupt, and disliked by the people they served. Positions were obtained by political appointment, and politics dominated promotion within the force. "Officers were primarily tools of local politicians," writes justice historian Samuel Walker (Senna 1996). In addition to pervasive brutality and corruption, the police did little to effectively prevent crime or provide public services. In those days, performing illegal and corrupt acts for politicians was a condition of continued employment.

Modern police practices were slow to evolve, and by the late 1800s, police boards and commissions had formed in an effort to reduce political influence and control over the police. In 1883, the Pendleton Act established the civil service, and political interference in police departments began to lessen. However, police departments continued to be under the control of local politicians, and the prevailing atmosphere was one of greed and corruption.

☯ Policing in the Twentieth Century

In 1893, the International Association of Chiefs of Police was formed, and during the first two decades of the twentieth century, it became the leading voice calling for the removal of political interference and control over the police. Banding together, the nation's chiefs demanded more autonomy in running their departments, and they proposed the formation of a centralized police structure and further civil service reform. Foremost among those calling for political independence was August Volmer, the chief of police in Berkeley, California, and O.W. Wilson, who reformed the Wichita, Kansas, police department in 1928. It was O.W. Wilson who brought modern management techniques to policing, and his famous book, *Police Administration,* became the most influential reference text on the subject (Wilson 1977).

From the 1920s to the 1960s, police departments evolved along highly militaristic lines and strived toward professionalism by relying on strict rules and regulations with heavy penalties for noncompliance in order to mold the conduct and behavior of police officers.

During the 1960s, the U.S. Supreme Court handed down decisions that greatly expanded the rights of suspects and had a dramatic effect on how police departments and individual police officers carried out their duties. *Mapp v. Ohio* (1961) placed strict guidelines on conducting searches and applied the exclusionary rule to state prosecutions. *Escobedo v. Illinois* (1964) provided defendants the right to an attorney during the course of any police interrogation. In *Miranda v. Arizona* (1966), the court required the police to advise suspects of their constitutional rights prior to questioning.

The civil rights movement and ensuing riots in New York, Detroit, and other cities, coupled with the student demonstrations during the Vietnam War, strained relations between the police and the public. Citizens began demanding more control over police agencies and civilian review boards began to pop up across the United States. Civilian control over police departments is still a hotly debated issue today.

During the 1980s and 1990s, institutionalized police corruption involving entire departments, which was common in early policing, became a rarity. However, corruption and unethical behavior are still problems in law enforcement, and their seriousness is perhaps best described by Patrick V. Murphy, former commissioner of the New York City Police Department, who expressed the following concerns (Goldstein 1975):

> For too long, corruption has been the skeleton in the police closet. Failure to discuss corruption openly has permitted it to flourish. A dearth of research on the subject handicaps police administrators, elected officials, journalists, and citizens anxious to address the problem of corruption.

> The reduction and control of police corruption can be complex. Many well-meaning police administrators have been unable to master the use of power, unable to obtain public support, and unable to control a large bureaucracy in ways sufficient to achieve substantial control of corruption. Holding top and middle management strictly accountable through the use of powerful sanctions is essential if the police administrator is to deal successfully with corruption and avoid the high risk of personal blame for its existence. Yet the environment engendered by the civil service mentality can protect the echelons immediately beneath the chief while the chief is held accountable for corruption. Therefore, despite civil service restraints, the chief must find ways to make his subordinates in management actively participate and hold them strictly accountable, for a positive approach to the control of corruption.

☯ ETHICAL PROBLEMS OF TODAY

Commissioner Murphy made those comments in 1975, and many would agree that little progress has been made since. Examples abound, but typical is a newspaper article featuring the following headline: "Officers Punished for Drinking Confiscated Keg" (Diehl-Dupont 1996). Apparently the police raided a party "where only one of the 75 or so youths present was over 21 years of age," dispersed those attending, and confiscated two kegs of beer. The alcohol was brought to police headquarters, where it was tagged as evidence. A sergeant, two veteran officers, two probationary police officers, and two civilian dispatchers apparently helped themselves to the beer. As a result of an internal investigation by the department, the chief of police suspended the sergeant for three weeks without pay. In a disciplinary letter to the sergeant, the chief is quoted in the article as saying, "Your behavior in this matter represents a complete abrogation of your responsibility as a supervisor and a leader in this organization. The fact that you not only engaged in such egregious behavior yourself, but also allowed sworn and civilian employee personnel . . . is despicable."

So, not only did the sergeant do a distinct disservice to himself and the department, his behavior influenced probationary police officers to engage in unethical conduct. Two of the other officers received one- and two-day suspensions without pay, while the others that were involved received a letter of reprimand that was placed in their personnel files. It is noteworthy that the police union is appealing the disciplinary action taken by the chief and that the suspensions won't be served until after all the administrative appeals are exhausted.

I thought it was disturbing that none of the officers were arrested and prosecuted or dismissed from the force and that the sergeant was not demoted in rank. Many would argue that the matter isn't serious enough to warrant criminal prosecution, termination from employment, or demotion in rank. Their position might be that no one was hurt, after all, and the situation was just a few police officers drinking beer on duty; it's not a case of a police officer brutally beating a suspect in handcuffs, taking a bribe, or intentionally lying in court; overall, it's a relatively minor matter.

It's not a minor matter! Even if we put aside the fact that the officers committed a criminal offense, the chief of police is correct in remarking that their unethical behavior "is despicable." Who have the officers harmed other than themselves? They have tarnished the badges of every single police officer across the United States, further eroded the trust the community places in its police officers, helped to reinforce the negative stereotypes many share about police officers, made it more difficult for citizens to embrace the profession as professional, and erased the effectiveness of many community programs in which police officers assist as role models for our children. The damage caused by these police officers "having a few beers" will take years to repair.

Another example occurred in Philadelphia. The *New York Times* reported in September of 1996 that the city had reached a court settlement in which it agreed to pay $3.5 million to forty-two plaintiffs resulting from "six officers pleading guilty to corruption charges" (Janofsky 1996). The article stated that "the settlements grew out of lawsuits filed and threatened by victims of the six officers" and that the "officers had been assigned to the 39th District, a collection of poor and working class inner-city neighborhoods with mostly black and Hispanic residents. Five of the officers were white; one was Asian." In addition to the monetary awards, a measure proposed in the settlement included the "creation of a permanent departmental position of integrity and accountability to oversee all aspects of ethical behavior, and the development of new procedures to help identify 'at risk' officers."

These are just two examples of what is occurring in police departments across the United States. Ethics matter, and perhaps it is time that we who wear the badge and carry the gun give greater emphasis to modeling our behavior along the lines suggested by General Fogleman.

> We expect all our members to live by the highest standards implicit in our core values: integrity, service before self, and commitment to excellence. We should not and will not accept less. However, when those standards are not met, then it is our responsibility and our duty to hold people involved accountable for their actions and respond appropriately.

☯ CODES OF ETHICS

Earlier in this text, ethics were defined as being primarily concerned with determining what is good for the individual and for society. The difficulty in defining what is good and how one should try to achieve it has to do with how people perceive what duty or obligation is owed to themselves and to one another. Philosophers have been debating for thousands of years whether there are objective standards that apply to everyone, and if what is good is known to all people (ethical absolutism), or whether individuals must decide what is good and what duty or obligation is owed to self or others based on each new situation (ethical reality).

Efforts to establish guidelines about what people should or should not do through codes of ethics, oaths of office, or codes of conduct probably began with the earliest forms of cuneiform writing in ancient Mesopotamia around 3200 B.C. However, the most widely known early code of conduct, the "Code of Hammurabi," was enacted by the Amorite ruler of the Babylonians somewhere around 1763 B.C. The code, discovered in 1901 during excavations in southern Persia, consisted of a mixture of 282 legal and ethical principles, mostly retaliatory in nature. The two most famous principles under the Code of Hammurabi are "an eye for an eye" and "let the buyer beware." The harshness of the code served as a point of departure from one of exact retaliation to the future development of justice under the Deuteronomic code, which forms the core of the biblical book of Deuteronomy. This and other parts of the Old Testament provided a Hebrew religious code in which religion and ethics are indissolubly united. The Deuteronomic code stressed the ideal of what is "just" by stressing such altruistic acts as generosity to the poor, help to the stranger, and fairness to children and elders. Typically codes of conduct seek to answer "what is right" or serve as guidelines for what people "ought" to do. Many establish penalties for behaviors thought to be wrong. The most widely known example of a code of conduct is the Ten Commandments, the laws recorded in the Bible (Exodus 20:1–17) as they were handed down from God to Moses on tablets of stone. The Ten Commandments are principally phrased in the negative, such as don't kill, don't lie, and don't steal. Yet, as is the case with many codes of conduct and ethics, no explanations are given to the individual as to how to apply these principles in real-life situations. Thus we are left to our own devices to determine if killing in self-defense or to save the life of another is permissible. Most codes are like this. They center on core values without providing a road map to traverse the difficult terrain of life. In other words, they don't spell out for a person how to do it.

A written or verbal commitment to the service to others beyond what is thought to be required by law or custom is often embodied in a code of ethics. Many are designed to regulate the actions of and set high standards for members of a specific profession. One of the best known codes of this type is the Hippocratic Oath. The Greek physician Hippocrates created a pledge for the medical profession in dedication to the preservation of life and the service of mankind. The Hippocratic Oath contains a wonderful mixture of statements combining ethics, religion, and logic at a time when superstition was paramount in men's minds. It is reprinted here in its entirety.

The Oath of Hippocrates

I swear by Apollo, the physician, and Asclepus and Health and All-Heal and all the gods and goddesses that, according to my ability and judgment, I will keep this oath and stipulation:

To reckon him who taught me this art equally dear to me as my parents, to share my substance with him and relieve his necessities if required; to regard his offspring as on the same footing with my own brothers, and to teach them this art if they should wish to learn it, without fee or stipulation, and that by precept, lecture and every other mode of instruction, I will impart a knowledge of the art to my own sons and to those of my teachers, and to disciples bound by a stipulation and oath, according to the law of medicine, but to none others.

I will follow that method of treatment which, according to my ability and judgment, I consider for the benefit of my patients and abstain from whatever is deleterious and mischievous. I will give no deadly medicine to anyone if asked, nor suggest any such counsel; furthermore I will not give to a woman an instrument to produce abortion.

With purity and with holiness I will pass my life and practice my art. I will not cut a person who is suffering from a stone, but will leave this to be done by practitioners of this work. Into whatever houses I enter I will go into them for the benefit of the sick and will abstain from every voluntary act of mischief and corruption; and further from the seduction of females or males; bond or free.

Whatever in connection with my professional practice, or not in connection with it, I may see or hear in the lives of men which ought not to be spoken abroad I will not divulge, as reckoning that all such should be kept secret.

While I continue to keep this oath unviolated may it be granted to me to enjoy life and the practice of the art, respected by all men at all times but should I trespass and violate this oath, may the reverse be true.

Other types of codes of ethics take a different approach. Rather than defining what a person should or shouldn't do, they define the person who adheres to the code or oath. Most codes of this type center on values thought to be vital to a person holding a specific office, title, rank, or professional status. A good example of this is the Boy Scout Oath and Law.

------------••●••------------

The Boy Scout Oath and Law

It is the mission of the Boy Scouts of America to serve others by helping to instill values in young people and, in other ways, to prepare them to make ethical choices over their lifetimes in achieving their full potential. The values we strive to instill are based on those found in the Scout Oath and Law:

Scout Oath

On my honor I will do my best
To do my duty to God and my country
    and to obey the Scout Law;
To help other people at all times;
To keep myself physically strong,
    mentally awake, and morally straight.

Scout Law

A Scout is Trustworthy	A Scout is Obedient
A Scout is Loyal	A Scout is Cheerful
A Scout is Helpful	A Scout is Thrifty
A Scout is Friendly	A Scout is Brave
A Scout is Courteous	A Scout is Clean
A Scout is Kind	A Scout is Reverent

Although each of us might interpret some of the semantics in the Scout Oath differently, such as what it is to be "morally straight," the point here is that the Scout Oath and Law aren't lists of what Scouts shouldn't do but what Scouts are.

☯ THE LAW ENFORCEMENT CODE OF ETHICS

In 1956, the California Peace Officers Association and the Peace Officers Research Association of California developed a law enforcement code of ethics that was adopted by the International Association of Chiefs of Police (IACP) at its 1957 conference. At that conference, the IACP also adopted the "Canons of Police Ethics." In the same tradition as the Scouts, the original police code of ethics goes beyond saying what a police officer should do; it defines what police officers are.

The Law Enforcement Code of Ethics

As a Law Enforcement Officer, my fundamental duty is to serve mankind; to safeguard lives and property; to protect the innocent against deception, the weak against oppression or intimidation, and the peaceful against violence or disorder; and to respect the Constitutional rights of all men to liberty, equality, and justice.

I will keep my private life unsullied as an example to all; maintain courageous calm in the face of danger, scorn, or ridicule; develop self-restraint; and be constantly mindful of the welfare of others. Honest in thought and deed in both my personal and official life, I will be exemplary in obeying the laws of the land and the regulations of my department. Whatever I see or hear of a confidential nature or that is confided to me in my official capacity will be kept ever secret unless revelation is necessary in the performance of my duty.

I will never act officiously or permit personal feelings, prejudices, animosities, or friendships to influence my decisions. With no compromise for crime and with relentless prosecution of criminals, I will enforce the law courteously and appropriately without fear or favor, malice, or ill will, never employing unnecessary force or violence and never accepting gratuities.

I recognize the badge of my office as a symbol of public faith, and I accept it as a public trust to be held so long as I am true to the ethics of police service. I will constantly strive to achieve these objectives and ideals, dedicating myself before God to my chosen profession . . . law enforcement.

Using the language in the "Law Enforcement Code of Ethics," we can create a model of what a police officer is.

A Police Officer Is

Concerned with the welfare of others
A protector of the weak and innocent
A model for others in public and private behavior
Brave, courageous, and bold
Loyal
Self-disciplined
Law abiding
Honest
Honorable
Pious
Trustworthy

--------------••●••-------------

Similar to the Scout Law, the words used in the "Law Enforcement Code of Ethics" and in the model are labels for values representing what occupational incumbents generally think are important. The "Canons of Police Ethics" was written to further define what police officers are and what they should and should not do. (The 1956 original version has not benefitted from the movement for inclusive language.) Following each article of the "Canons of Police Ethics" is a commentary further explaining the meaning behind each section.

Canons of Police Ethics

Article I.   Primary Responsibility of Job

The primary responsibility of the police service, and of the individual officer, is the protection of the people of the United States through the upholding of their laws; chief among these is the Constitution of the United States and its amendments. The law enforcement officer always respects the whole of the community and its legally expressed will and is never the arm of any political party or clique.

Commentary: All police officers took an oath to uphold the laws enumerated in the Constitution. This article reminds us that the role of the police in a democracy is one of protector of all the people in the community. Police services to the poor, the oppressed, the weak, and those who cannot help themselves must be of the same quality as those given to the rich, the powerful, the titled, and the privileged. Further, the police must remain apart from even the appearance of being used by or holding allegiance to a particular political party.

Article II.   Limitations of Authority

The first duty of a law enforcement officer, as upholder of the law, is to know its bounds upon him in enforcing it. Because he represents the legal will of the community, be it local, state, or federal, he must be aware of the limitations and proscriptions which the people, through law, have placed upon him. He must recognize the genius of the American system of government which gives to no man, groups of men, or institutions, absolute power, and he must insure that he, as a prime defender of the system, does not pervert its character.

Commentary: The first part of this article tells us that as police officers we are lifelong students of the law. Since the law and how it is enforced continually change, police officers have an obligation to have a thorough understanding of not just its application but its intent. The second part of this article is a warning to police officers not to allow any person or group to use the police to further personal interests. The role of the police is to gather facts to prove innocence just as much as guilt. Thus, the police must not only be impartial, but defend that impartiality from those who would use an officer to achieve personal vengeance, gain, or power over others.

I remember several occasions when attorneys employed by the state's criminal justice system (prosecutors, state attorneys, and district attorneys) attempted to advise me or those working for me that the police worked for them. When this happened, I quickly pointed out that to the contrary, we worked with them, not for them. The difference between the two is that the police role is not to obtain evidence with which to prosecute people, but to obtain and report the facts (both for and against a defendant) for any person or institution that wishes to review them. In a democracy, this distinct separation of roles is very important.

Article III. Duty to be Familiar with the Law and with Responsibilities of Self and Other Public Officials

The law enforcement officer shall assiduously apply himself to the study of the principles of the laws which he is sworn to uphold. He will make certain of his responsibilities in the particulars of their enforcement, seeking aid from his superiors in matters of technicality or principles when these are not clear to him; he will make special effort to fully understand his relationship to other public officials, including other law enforcement agencies, particularly on matters of jurisdiction, both geographically and substantively.

Commentary: If Article II wasn't clear enough, Article III hammers home the point that the margin of error for a police officer is minimal. When mistakes are made at the company or factory, most often money is lost. When a police officer makes a mistake, people lose their life or liberty. It is not enough to merely know what the law says and blindly apply it across the board in all situations. The police officer must understand the basis of the law. A good example here is the exclusionary rule—evidence illegally obtained by the police cannot be used against a defendant at trial. This section of the code also recognizes the importance of community standards and jurisdictions by pointing out that in a democracy the duties of the police are separate from those of the courts and legislature. Similarly, police jurisdiction and enforcement powers often end at the town or city limits, depending on the type of incident. Officers have an obligation to be familiar with laws and regulations relative to this.

Article IV. Utilization of Proper Means to Gain Proper Ends

The law enforcement officer shall be mindful of his responsibility to pay strict heed to the selection of means of discharging the duties of his office. Violations of law or disregard for public safety and property on the part of the officer are intrinsically wrong; they are self-defeating in that they instill in the public mind a like disposition. The employment of illegal means, no matter how worthy the end, is certain to encourage disrespect for the law and the officers. If the law is to be honored, it must first be honored by those who enforce it.

Commentary: This section deals with two important principles of law enforcement. First, the police are held to at least the same standards as any other citizen. Only in specific exigent circumstances is it permissible for a police officer to speed, double-park, go through red traffic signals, and so on. Second, the police cannot use illegal means to catch crooks. We discussed the "Dirty Harry syndrome" earlier: the ends do not justify the means. The police cannot violate the law to uphold it—no illegal wiretaps; no searches of persons, places, or things; no planting of evidence; and no coerced confessions in order to solve a crime.

Article V. Cooperation with Public Officials in the Discharge of their Authorized Duties

The law enforcement officer shall cooperate fully with public officials in the discharge of authorized duties, regardless of party affiliation or personal prejudice. He shall be meticulous, however, in assuring himself of the propriety, under the law, of such actions and shall guard against the use of his office or person, whether knowingly or unknowingly, in any improper or illegal action. In any situation open to question, he shall seek authority from his superior officers, giving him a full report of the proposed service or action.

Commentary: Is it OK for a police officer to assist in the enforcement of eviction notices, forcing people out of their homes? Isn't that a civil matter? Is it permissible for a police officer to be on duty outside an area where people are coming to vote? How about being present when a wrecker tows a car for a credit company because the owner hasn't made the payments? Is it right for the police to assist a woman or man in getting her or his furniture after a divorce? This section recognizes that the police do become involved in these types of situations that often involve other agencies in the criminal justice system, both civil and criminal. It acknowledges that the perception of the public may be that the police are being used in an inappropriate manner. In such cases, officers have an obligation to make certain their role is firmly grounded in law, proper, and falls within the prescribed guidelines of their department.

Article VI. Private Conduct

The law enforcement officer shall be mindful of his special identification by the public as an upholder of the law. Laxity of conduct or manner in private life, expressing either disrespect for the law or seeking to gain special privilege, cannot but reflect upon the officer and the police service. The community and the service require that the law enforcement officer lead the life of a decent and honorable man. Following the career of a policeman gives no man special perquisites.

It does give the satisfaction of pride of following and furthering an unbroken tradition of safeguarding the American republic. The officer who reflects upon this tradition will not degrade it. Rather, he will so conduct his private life that the public will regard him as an example of stability, fidelity, and morality.

Commentary: Wearing the badge and carrying the gun gives no one special privileges. On the contrary, it imposes special obligations. A police officer cannot break the law on or off duty. Further, a police officer must ensure that no one would even have the perception that he or she is breaking the law: no gifts from merchants at Christmas, no free or discounted meals, no special seating at movies and sporting events, not even a free cup of coffee, on or off duty. Police officers do not use profanity, smoke in public while in uniform, put their hands in their pockets, drink alcohol to excess when off duty, or use any illicit substance. The list goes on, but you get the picture. If you can't discipline yourself to not do these things, you still don't understand that policing is a way of life, not a job.

Article VII. Conduct Toward the Public

The law enforcement officer, mindful of his responsibility to the whole community, shall deal with individuals of the community in a manner calculated to instill respect for its laws and its police service. The law enforcement officer shall conduct his official life in a manner such as will inspire confidence and trust. Thus, he will be neither overbearing nor subservient, as the individual citizen has neither an obligation to stand in awe of him nor a right to command him. The officer will give service where he can and require compliance with the law. He will do neither from personal preference or prejudice but only as a duly appointed officer of the law discharging his sworn obligation.

Commentary: An officer must treat every person with dignity and respect. As a servant of all the people, the police officer cannot be influenced by wealth, power, prestige, or position in the delivery of police services.

Article VIII. Conduct in Arresting and Dealing with Law Violators

The law enforcement officer shall use his powers of arrest strictly in accordance with the law and with due regard to the rights of the citizen concerned. His office gives him no right to prosecute the violator nor to mete out punishment for the offense. He shall, at all times, have a clear appreciation of his responsibilities and limitations regarding detention of the violator; he shall conduct himself in such a manner as will minimize the possibility of having to use force. To this end he shall cultivate a dedication to the service of the people and the equitable upholding of their laws whether in the handling of law violators or in dealing with the law-abiding.

Commentary: Regardless of a police officer's personal feelings, force must be used only after all other ways of handling a situation have been tried and failed. Even then, only the barest minimum amount of force necessary may be used, and it must cease when compliance is obtained.

Article IX. Gifts and Favors

The law enforcement officer, representing the government, bears the heavy responsibility of maintaining in his own conduct, the honor and integrity of all government institutions. He shall, therefore, guard against placing himself in a position in which any person can reasonably assume that special consideration is being given. Thus, he should be firm in refusing gifts, favors, or gratuities, large or small, which can, in the public mind, be interpreted as capable of influencing his judgment in the discharge of his duties.

Commentary: Do not accept any gift, favor, special privilege, handout, or even so much as a pencil from anyone, regardless of the circumstances, or give the perception that you do or would.

Article X. Presentation of Evidence

The law enforcement officer shall be concerned equally in the prosecution of the wrongdoer and the defense of the innocent. He shall ascertain what constitutes evidence and shall present such evidence impartially and without malice. In so doing, he will ignore social, political, and other distinctions among the persons involved, strengthening the tradition of the reliability and the integrity of an officer's word.

The law enforcement officer shall take special pains to increase his perception and skill of observation, mindful that in many situations his is the solo impartial testimony to the facts of a crime.

Commentary: As mentioned earlier, the police have as much an obligation to gather facts supporting a person's innocence as they do his or her guilt. Further, this section reminds a police officer of the duty to report all evidence, even if such evidence would allow a hardened criminal to go free and no matter if the suspect is of a different class, color, religion, sex, or political party affiliation from the officer. Those who enforce the law must do so equally for all persons. Officers are urged to become experts in their chosen profession and make every effort to increase their skill level in recognition of their special role as independent investigator of fact.

Article XI. Attitude Toward Profession

The law enforcement officer shall regard the discharge of his duties as a public trust and recognize his responsibility as a public servant. By diligent study and sincere attention to self-improvement he shall strive to make the best possible application of science to the solution of crime and, in the field of human relationships, strive for effective leadership and public influence in matters affecting public safety. He shall appreciate the importance and responsibility of his office, hold police work to be an honorable profession rendering valuable service to his community and country.

Commentary: This article clearly acknowledges the tremendous power given to the police in a democratic society—the power to detain, arrest, and even kill, under certain circumstances. It reminds us that the police organization is service oriented and that with great power comes the responsibility to use it wisely and sparingly. If officers strive to be deserving of high respect, prestige, autonomy, and fair remuneration, then the public trust must be earned each and every day.

The "Law Enforcement Code of Ethics" and the "Canons of Police Ethics" do much more than just serve as boundaries to restrict the motives and behavior of police officers. They establish what police officers are and the core values inherent in the profession. They recognize that because of the immense power given to the police by society, police officers must attend to the actions of other police officers and those who would use the police to further their own ends. Because of the unique nature of police services, the police officer's day is packed with decisions, some of which may make a difference in people's lives forever. Decisions often require choices between alternative courses of action. The code does not allow an officer to stand amid evil and do nothing. It requires an active commitment to justice. This type of commitment requires officers to not tolerate those among them who do not live up to the standards of honesty, integrity, and honor established in the code.

CHAPTER 4

Personal and Professional Development

"All that we are is the result of what we have thought. The mind is everything. What we think, we become."

Buddha

☯ THE PATH TO THE WAY

This part of the book concerns itself primarily with personal and professional development. It's written for those who wish to explore the high road, away from the cloud of dust thrown up by the thundering herd. Nothing of special merit comes from mainstream thinking. To change the way we think or modify long-established patterns of behavior, tremendous effort is required. It's easier to just allow ourselves to be carried along by the pull of the tide than to take the risk of swimming toward a particular shore where new adventures are waiting.

Let's begin by rediscovering the way to the path through the outlining of an ancient philosophy that the sands of time have all but buried. The philosophy embraces the same code of honor and way of life of King Arthur Pendragon's Knights of the Round Table, the Three Musketeers, Zorro, and the Lone Ranger. The Green Berets, Navy Seals, the French Foreign Legion, some religious orders, and a few military academies use parts of its precepts today. I call this way of life the "path of the *warrior*," and in bygone days its principles were passed from veteran cops to young rookies as they walked a beat together. In a far-off place in long ago time, when the claw and fang ruled within the clan, fathers used to pass these secrets through blood oaths to their sons. And, since the days of the beat cop are all but finished and my shield is battered and worn, I hand the baton, the code, and the light to you. Follow this path if you are to be a *warrior* and share your light with others. But tread carefully! We become what we pretend to be!

To become a *warrior* you must turn your back on the consensus of others, open the gate, cross the bridge, and begin an *inner* quest of your heart and spirit. There is no instant transformation, but all of us have the capacity to mold ourselves into something new. You can't change your past behavior, but you can learn from it. The process of becoming a *warrior* and transforming your inner self works from the inside out. You must adopt the motto of Delphi and "know thyself." Every human being has boundaries, invisible lines that control our inner selves. We have to take risks in order to change and grow. *Warriors* possess a heightened consciousness of the worth of their past experiences and the ability to turn them into new outlooks for the future.

> *Our greatest glory is not in never failing,*
> *but in rising every time we fail.*
>
> Confucius

☯ WARRIOR PHILOSOPHY

There are ten primary virtues that all *warriors* possess and must continuously seek to develop and sustain. The ten primary virtues of a *warrior* are self-discipline, wisdom, courage, faith, honor, virtue, mercy, compassion, purity of heart, and freedom of spirit. To become a *warrior,* you must develop a strong inner spirit to draw upon when encountering the difficult and painful obstacles interwoven along the path to the way. What we are is a result of what we think and what we do. "One never does wrong by doing right." *Warriors* possess special powers unique to their tribe because they have developed and use these qualities in the service of others. The pounding of the drums along the path to the way releases powerful forces for good, but the dark side is also very strong. It lurks at every bend in the path, always present, forever watching for the dark night of the soul and signs of weakness in a *warrior's* armor. By developing inner strength you will be able to share your light and contribute to the growth of others.

All growth requires change and the use of positive energy. Every *warrior* has an outward and an inward journey along the path to the way. Change requires risk. To change and face the risk of growing requires courage. Courage is the willingness to confront fear. Beware! It's a long and difficult journey, and fewer are reaching the light to sing the song of joy at the end of the path.

There is nothing noble in being superior to some other man.
The true nobility is in being superior to your previous self.

Hindustani proverb

You know you have been in the presence of a true *warrior* when your inner light glows brighter. I call this sharing a form of growth because it creates more light, not less. Energy and light can be infinitely expanded by discovering new and different ways to think and live. The light allows you to explore the darkness, examine what is there, and discard behaviors that do not contribute to your well-being.

You must give yourself permission to be your own hero. This new you is often disturbing to people who have an interest in controlling your behavior. People often feel threatened by anyone different from themselves.

The inner spirit, or indwelling, of a person who has chosen to walk the path of a *warrior* is protected by armor gathered before and after unlocking the gate opening the path to the way. Armor is created by forging together self-discipline, integrity, righteousness, honor, and love. All care-givers are motivated by love for others. I've often thought that the time-honored tradition of police officers' willingly stepping in harm's way to protect others is a wonderful example of love in action. The words of Alfred Tennyson in "The Charge of the Light Brigade" bring a strong image of love in action to my mind.

Cannon to the right of them,
Cannon to the left of them,
Cannon in front of them
Volley'd and thunder'd;
Storm'd at with shot and shell,
Boldly they rode and well,
Into the jaws of Death,
Into the mouth of Hell
Rode the six hundred.

The greatest and most impenetrable armor is love. Love is the furnace that produces the fire to forge the mettle from which powerful armor and shields are created. Nothing is superior to love when attacking that which is strong and unyielding. Love gathers strength with patience. In order to be happy we must love others, but first we must love ourselves and treat ourselves with respect.

Things that sustain the body, mind, and spirit are shields that *warriors* use to strengthen and protect their inner spirit. Exercise restores the body, education and life experiences nourish the mind, and prayer lifts up the spirit. A *warrior* uses specific qualities or traits in the service of others. Hope, trustworthiness, duty, benevolence, mercy, compassion, kindness, innocence, and a thirst for justice are the traits of a *warrior*.

It's not easy to become a *warrior*. It's even more difficult to remain a *warrior* after becoming one. Many answer the call of the drums, but few are able to sustain the strength of character necessary to march to them. There are many labyrinths, traps, and dragons along the path to the way.

You must scale the mountains if you are to view the plains.

Chinese philosopher

Courage and inner fortitude are required to overcome the difficult and sometimes painful obstacles along the path a *warrior* must travel. Abuse of power and self-diminishing behavior are traps that snare and draw a would-be *warrior* off the path. We are often seduced by illusions of power bestowed upon us by the titles, promotions, or credentials we receive. These outward symbols quickly lose their luster unless placed on a foundation of self-worth. Because we often close our hearts to the people in our lives, many would-be *warriors* suffer the penalty of loneliness while surrounded by heaps of gold. Temptation and suffering for the sake of others are tests each person on the path to becoming a *warrior* must face. The voice and comfort of the herd is loud and strong. Although a *warrior* is sometimes joined by others, the walk is often the high and lonely path of the nomad. True *warriors* do not cower at the opinions of others, but feel themselves accountable to a higher tribunal than man.

All who walk the path have the freedom to choose where their steps will take them. There are many different paths but only one "way."

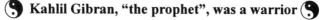

Kahlil Gibran, "the prophet", was a warrior

Warriors accept total responsibility for their thoughts, behaviors, deeds, and actions. This is known as decision making. *Warriors* heed the wisdom of Omar of Persia, the Sufi mystic, who said:

There are four things that come not back

> The spoken word
> The sped arrow
> The past life
> The neglected opportunity

Sometimes a person walking the path of a *warrior* will lose one of the shields guarding his or her armor to a trap or dragon. Dragons are a *warrior*'s worst enemy. They are powerful, almost as powerful as a full-fledged *warrior*. Alcohol and other drugs, greed and malice, envy and negative thinking infect the blood and weaken the spirit of a would-be *warrior*. Others' voices are often very loud, and they drown out the pounding of the drums.

You must learn to listen to your inner voice to choose a guardian along the path to the way. If a *warrior* is pure of heart, sometimes a guardian along the path to the way will share a shield in the form of wisdom or grace with a person who has lost one to a trap or a dragon. *Warriors* seek out these champions in order to radiate in the glow of their light. A warrior-guardian's shield is magical; it casts light in the dark when approached by a dragon disguised in the gloom of despair, powerlessness, or adversity.

A true warrior-guardian helps those walking the path in their seeking of life, health, power over themselves, knowledge, wisdom, virtue, and love. Doctors, teachers, those who care for the aged, nurses, firemen, coaches, and police officers are among those who have unlocked the gate to the path of a *warrior* for others.

Warrior-guardians are bridges composed of activating energy. Your energy dramatically increases when you come into contact with a *warrior* transformed into a guardian. However, if what you're seeking is power and control over other people, prestige, glory, or money, a guardian cannot give this to you. A guardian along the path to the way

 Ghandi and Albert Schweitzer were warriors ☯

can only guide you to the passageway, help you open the gate, and sustain you on your pilgrimage leading to the priceless gems of inner peace, knowing, joy, and love.

A rainbow is a group of true *warriors* who have gathered together to light the path and pound the drums so "shooting stars" and "comets" can find their shadows and their way back to the path. Prayer to a higher power, a family with joined hands, little children, grandmothers, and angels can cause a rainbow to gather and very powerful magic to be released. There is an inner and outer connection between what you do and how you feel about yourself.

Too many material things make it difficult for a *warrior* to focus on the path to the way. Many become prisoners of too much substance. The material world causes a heavy mist to form over the path, blurring a *warrior*'s vision and distorting the sound of the pounding drums. Better to give to others that which you do not need so as to be able to move quickly around dragons and jump over and avoid traps.

If a man empties his purse into his head,
no one can take it from him.

Benjamin Franklin

Laughter is considered to be full of magic. It restores and sustains the spirit of a *warrior*. Dragons disguised in worry, doubt, or despair cannot break through a shield formed of laughter. Giving is the foundation of a *warrior*'s work. The act of giving brightens a *warrior*'s glow. Taking saps a *warrior*'s energy. All troubles cease when basking in the light resulting from giving to others. Giving of self opens a transparent doorway in the path and forms a talisman that allows a *warrior* to become invisible and pass through dragons and over traps.

Joy is a *warrior*'s companion along the path to the way. Ego and envy are jackals snapping at a *warrior*'s heels. It does not take a very brave dog to bark at the bones of a lion, so jackals attack *warriors* in hordes, hoping to wear them down.

☯ **Joan of Arc and Winston Churchill were warriors** ☯

The songs of birds, water rippling over a stone in a brook, wind rustling through the trees, the tinkling of a bell, the ringing of wind chimes, and the laughter of little children are all music to a *warrior*. Dragons and traps cannot harm a *warrior* listening to this music. The sight of any animal in a forest causes a *warrior* to pause, and sometimes you can stand next to such a *warrior* for a moment and bask in his or her light. A return to the harmony of nature always refreshes a *warrior*'s energy. Water, wind, earth, and fire are a *warrior*'s amulets. All *warriors* on the path carry a sacramental, such as a scapular, a picture of a loved one, or an object, that has special meaning for them.

Good deeds without reward expand a *warrior*'s light. If a reward is received, the light dims and no deed has been done. Since all that we are is a product of our thoughts, *warriors* guard the mind from the dark side, seeking the stillness, harmony, and peace of mind created by the power of moving toward the light.

Warrior heed the wisdom of the Serbian sage:

Be humble, for the worst thing in the world is of the same
stuff as you; be confident,
for the stars are of the same stuff as you.

A PRACTICAL GUIDE FOR TODAY'S WARRIOR

 Bushido: The way of the warrior; a code of ethical behavior founded on humility, honor, and discipline

There are many who wear the badge and carry the gun who are not yet peacekeepers and lack the attributes necessary to become care-givers. Passing some tests, graduating from a police academy, taking an oath of office, and receiving a badge and a gun, does not make a person a cop. They may have the symbols of the office and wear the uniform but still not have embraced the code of a *warrior*.

Asked what their primary job is, most will answer "to arrest people who have committed crimes." Yet if that were true, almost anyone could do the job. With a few exceptions, arresting people is easy and takes no special skill or talent. Statistically, less than two percent of a police officer's time is spent arresting people for having committed a crime. Rather, intervening and making a difference in other people's lives is what policing and care-giving is all about. I call this intervening and making a difference in people's lives "sharing the light."

Why is sharing the light so important? It's important because achievement, inner peace, happiness, and joy is obtained only through our relationships with others, spiritual guidance, and inner strength. In order to be able to share your light with others and receive the grace of inner peace, you must walk the path of a *warrior*. Reflect for a moment on the words of Theodore Roosevelt, who offered a good definition of those walking the path of a *warrior*.

> The credit belongs to the persons who are actually in the arena; those whose face is marred by dust and sweat and blood; who strives valiantly; who errs and comes short again and again; who knows the great enthusiasms, the great devotions, and spend themselves in a worthy cause; who, at the best, knows in the end the triumph of high achievement; and who, at the worst, fails while daring greatly, so that their place will never be with those cold and timid souls who know neither victory nor defeat.

So, how is it actually done, this walking the path of a *warrior*? What is required? How long does it take? How will I know if I've done it? Why do so many fail? The answers to these questions are easy, yet complicated. When I entered my first karate *dojo,* my *sensei* asked me what it was that I was seeking. I answered that I wanted a black belt.

He untied his black belt, handed it to me, and said, "Here's a black belt. What can you do with it?"

Other than using it to fasten my karate *gi,* there wasn't much I could do with it. Nothing of lasting value comes easily. I was to later learn that the black belt is merely a symbol of a lifelong pilgrimage along a specific path. Karate is another form of education. Education is about self-discovery and self-control.

So, let's begin your journey with a map for you to follow consisting of words and symbols that have meaning only if you allow them to. One of the things that makes *warriors* different from other people is the energy of their inner spirit and the armor they forge to strengthen and protect the energy. Because of what police officers routinely see and do, a certain amount of psychological hardiness is required. Police officers often experience or are later involved in traumatic events that occur at lightning speed. Since policing is a doing profession, the horror of what's occurring (perhaps a fatal accident involving children who have burned to death or a fellow officer who is badly assaulted when effecting an arrest) is placed in the background of the mind so the *warrior* can function and perform whatever service to others is required. The physical and psychological effects of experiencing traumatic events cause what I call a wound to the soul, or the inner spirit. The area around the wound hardens in order to protect the mind and allow the *warrior* to function, but this hardening eventually weakens, leaving the warrior vulnerable to dragons and traps. Too many wounds to the soul often result in overwhelming stress. Many *warriors* fall from the path and seek an easing of the pain in the form of alcohol, drugs, and other self-diminishing behaviors. That's why the life expectancy of our warriors is so low, the divorce rate so high, and so many are living lives of quiet desperation.

It doesn't have to be that way! William James, the famous philosopher-psychologist, thought the most significant finding in this century is that "human beings can alter their lives by altering their attitudes of mind." Those who are able to consistently walk the path of a *warrior* understand the importance of protecting their inner spirit. Your inner spirit is the core of your being. It's what makes you special and different from other people. Just as no two snowflakes are alike yet consist only of crystallized water, no two people are exactly alike. Your inner spirit is formed in great part by how you interpret your past experiences and by the dialogue you have with yourself in your own mind. Starting this very instant, you can decide to strengthen your indwelling and make positive choices about how you will live.

Who decides whether you are happy or unhappy? You do! People who feel good about themselves, about their self-worth and their abilities, achieve greater results. People with little self-respect don't

 Ivanhoe and Sir Galahad were warriors

treat themselves or others with respect. Many people live their lives in a perpetual state of planning for future happiness. They are not living with a sense of joy now but will when they receive that promotion, or on their birthday, or at Christmas, or when they get whatever it is they have convinced themselves is meaningful. Or, as Ralph Waldo Emerson put it, "we are always getting ready to live, but never living."

Warriors train themselves to live in the present by getting in touch with their *tan-tien,* or *chi.* Your *chi* is your inner energy, the center oracle that joins the body, mind, and spirit into the uniqueness of who you are. *Warriors* live in harmony with themselves and everything around them by continuously disciplining themselves to do the things necessary to strengthen their body, mind, and spirit. How do you strengthen your body, mind, and spirit? Well, think of yourself in terms of a triangle with three sides of even length that support one another. If all three legs are strong, the triangle stands firm, the tension and strength of each side firmly bonding with the others. However, if one of the legs weakens, the triangle begins to sag, requiring the other two legs to work harder to support it. If more than one leg weakens, the triangle collapses into itself.

The ancient Greeks used the triangle to represent the harmony that must exist between the body, mind, and spirit for people to function at their highest level. Those walking the path of a *warrior* consistently do the things necessary to build, grow, and sustain the sides of the triangle of life containing their inner *chi.*

☯ THE INNER SPIRIT OF A WARRIOR

I don't know anyone who has a vibrant, radiating, inner spirit who hasn't entered into a personal relationship with and dedicated the service they render to others to God. I know that's not what you expected to read here, but if you examine your inner heart you know it to be true. Which God? Does it really matter? Many different languages, but the same prayer; different prayers, but the same God. The music changes, but the melody stays the same. Faith is the light of the soul and food for the inner spirit. Or, as Norman Vincent Peale wrote, "Faith in God, faith in other people, faith in yourself, faith in life." You were created for a specific purpose, and I believe that as a police officer you are "the peacekeeper," blessed, and a soldier of God.

Finding out what your purpose is and dedicating your life to it is my definition of joy.

The words we choose to speak to ourselves have a direct effect on the way we think and the way in which we choose to live and behave. Our conscious thoughts begin the moment we wake up and often shape the way we *choose* to live our day. When you awaken, begin each new day of your life with these words:

Today is the day the Lord has made, I will rejoice and be glad.

If God is on my side, who can prevail against me?

Sound a little corny to you? A little different? Soft and un*warrior*like, perhaps? Well, consider Peter, the disciple of Christ known as the "Rock." I suspect Peter was hard as nails but knew a good thing when he saw it. In order to develop the attributes of a *warrior*—discipline over self, wisdom, courage, faith, virtue, mercy, compassion, purity of heart, and freedom of spirit—it's necessary to build a strong foundation of faith: the assurance of things hoped for, the proving of things unseen. Your conscience, or inner custodian if you prefer, enables you to distinguish right from wrong. When the pounding of the drums is strong, follow the sound and you will always be on the side of the just. But remember, good and bad judgments about things of the earthly world are usually based on your own personal preferences.

The awesome, discretionary powers given to you as a police officer by society enable you to make a significant difference in the lives of the people you swore to serve and protect. Power is neutral. It can be used for good or evil. Put your faith in God, treat the people you serve like they are members of your own family, show compassion and mercy in all of your works, and you will have peace of mind and purity of heart.

When I was commander of the Hartford, Connecticut, Police SWAT team, each of us carried a small plastic packet containing a card which listed our blood type, the phone number of our next of kin, and the name of the hospital we wanted to be taken to if we were shot. On the reverse side of this packet, most of us carried a scapular or a medal of Michael the Archangel. We didn't spend a lot of time talking about religion with one another; we simply tried to model behavior that reflected the *warrior* within us in a spiritual way. If God was on our side, who could prevail against us?

To give you a concrete, practical example of how to build your inner spirit, here's one of the ways I do it. About once every six months, I travel to a nearby monastery to attend a retreat that offers a program of prayer and meditation. It's understood that with the exception of mass and meals everyone has taken a vow of silence. I'm shown to a small room on the first floor that has a cot, bathroom, and one small bureau. The walls are bare with the exception of a crucifix. I usually stay twenty-four hours. During that time, I walk the spacious grounds, pray, fast, and go to mass. I ask myself some basic questions:

➢ Who am I?

➢ What things are most important in my life?

➢ How is my relationship going with my wife and children? What can I do to make those relationships better?

➢ What is it that I want?

➢ What are my goals for the next six months? a year from now? five years from now? What will I do to achieve them?

➢ What is it that God would have me do?

➢ Am I happy?

➢ When was the last time I experienced a sense of joy in my life?

➢ What have I done to strengthen my relationship with the Lord?

➢ Am I a better person today than I was yesterday?

Obviously you don't have to go to a monastery to ask yourself these questions. A long walk in the woods, on the beach, or across the prairie or desert will do just fine. All you really need is a quiet place to retreat to and the ability to be completely honest with yourself. Sustain and strengthen your inner spirit by going to church, reading the Bible, talking with God every day, erasing all negative thoughts from your mind, and praying for guidance. All who walk the path of a *warrior* do these things. If *you* do them, I promise it will change your life!

☯ AN ENCOUNTER WITH A MONK FROM THE OLD WORLD: ANCIENT SKILLS

The first person I met outside of law enforcement whom I considered to be a warrior-guardian was a monk. My doctoral program required attendance at several seminars given across the country by adjunct faculty in a variety of disciplines. I had put off fulfilling the requirement that I attend a course in qualitative and quantitative analysis (of course, dreadful stuff) and ended up at a seminar at the Hilton Hotel in Atlanta, Georgia, because it was the last one being offered that semester. At the same time this doctoral seminar was going on, another group at the hotel was attending a religious convention sponsored by the Byzantine Rite of the Catholic Church. An information booth about its conference was located in the lobby, and out of curiosity I picked up a brochure.

One of the lectures being offered was strangely titled: "People Are More Important Than Things." Directly under the title were the words "A discussion with a monk of the Eastern Church." As I sat through several lectures with my fellow doctoral candidates, my mind kept drifting back to those words: "People Are More Important Than Things." A simple sentence that conveys a message everyone knows. Nothing new there, yet I found myself writing that sentence over and over again in my notebook and looking for more meaning behind the words. I couldn't think of anything of special significance other than the obvious. Leafing through the brochure again, I found that the monk's lecture was seven until eight-thirty that evening.

"What in the world are they going to discuss for an hour and a half?" I mumbled to myself. Our seminar concluded at 5 P.M., and after dinner, for some unexplained reason, I found myself heading toward the hotel's Granada Room, where the monk was going to hold his discussion. I was surprised to find a large group of people of all ages and races crowding into the room. Children, teenagers, young adults, those in the prime of life, and the aged were gathered together, and everyone seemed to be in animated conversation. I could hear Arabic, French, Hebrew, Italian, and English being spoken. The air was charged with anticipation and excitement. Little children were running up and down the aisles, joining first one group, then another, and receiving smiled greetings at each one, all understood through smiles and laughter. I didn't know what to make of it. The place had the atmosphere of a wedding reception.

I looked for a seat on the aisle so I could make a quick departure if the discussion turned out to be a disaster. Up close to the front was the last one, and I sat down next to a man about my own age. He was leaning forward and speaking in Arabic to a woman across the aisle. Sensing my discomfort at having landed in the path of their conversation, he turned to me, smiled, and extended his hand, saying, "Good evening, my brother. You are here to listen to the sage?"

The enunciation of his English was better than my own. "The sage?" I replied.

"Yes. Father Nicholas. The one who is speaking here this evening." He leaned closer, raising his eyebrows and lowering his voice. "Don't you know who he is?"

I searched my mind for something intelligent to say, but could only muster, "No, I've never heard of him. I just saw this brochure and thought I'd drop by."

I felt even more awkward and held up the brochure as evidence. For a fleeting moment, I thought about excusing myself and leaving. Obviously everyone in the room knew who this monk was but me.

However, my new-found friend tried again, introducing himself as Girard and saying, "You're in for a real treat. Father Nicholas is an unusual man. We're fortunate to have him back in America with us for a time."

"In America?" I asked.

"Yes, yes. He has been in prison in the Middle East for the past six years, and now he is back, and the people are in dire need of him."

I glanced at my watch and noticed that the monk was ten minutes late. All of a sudden, the throng became quiet, and the people began making their way to their seats. A little old man with a long white beard had taken a seat at a table in the front of the room. He was dressed in a simple black frock with a hood, a white rope looped around the middle for a belt, and leather sandals. He picked up a small portable microphone and hooked the battery pack to the rope belt.

He stood awkwardly and, with a slight smile on his face and twinkle in his eye, stepped forward. In a deep, rich voice he said, "Let us begin. How many of you slept in a bed last night?"

All of us raised our hands.

"In your lifetimes, has any person in this audience not had a place to sleep for the night?"

No answer.

"In your lifetimes, has any of you gone without clothing?"

No answer.

"Has any of you gone for more than a day without anything to eat or drink?"

No answer.

"Two days?"

No answer.

"Then thank the Lord, all of you have everything you need. Anything else is extra and you should praise the Lord for your abundance. Go, love one another, and love God with all of your heart, soul, and mind."

He then gave a little wave to the audience, sat down, and folded his hands, lecture concluded.

A murmur swelled through the audience. A man stood a few rows behind me and said, "But Abba (father in Arabic), isn't there more to life than just that? Even the animals have a place to sleep, food to eat, and water to drink. Are we to want nothing else?"

The old monk stood up again.

"You forgot the God part, but that's OK. What more are you are seeking, my son?"

The man from the audience said, "I came here to learn from you about how to be . . . happy. How to live a life of joy. I have studied the scriptures and ancient books all of my life. I follow all of the rules. I hurt no one. But I am not very happy. What more should I do?"

The monk shook his head and laughed. "First, stop reading the scriptures so much. Just meditate on the Lord's Prayer. The rest is commentary, ancient history, and repetition. Remember the saying of the sage, 'We see things as we are, not as they are.' The qualities of your thoughts define your inner happiness. If you would be happy, train your mind to think happy thoughts. The Dalai Lama said, 'We live very close together. So our prime purpose in this life is to help others. And if you can't help, at least don't hurt them.'"

The old monk gave a kind of salute with his hand toward the man and finished by saying, "The rest is up to you. You are responsible for your own thoughts and thus your own happiness."

A woman rose from the audience and said to the monk, "Abba, my son is living in sin and is not following the commandments. He lives with a woman who is not his wife. What should I do?"

He shrugged his shoulders. "I don't understand your question."

The woman's eyes grew wide, and she looked around the room as if the monk were senile. She repeated her question. "My son is not following the teachings of our church, and I worry about his soul. What should I do?"

The old monk wagged a finger at the woman saying, "What your son is doing is between him and God. Not between me, you, him, and

God. He will find his own way in his own time. You must have faith and do the same. Live your life, and let your son live his."

A young man, about fifteen years old, rose from the audience. "Abba, I have cancer. They say I have only a few months to live, and I'm afraid to die. Will Jesus save me?"

The monk called the young man forward to where he was standing, embraced him, and then turned back to the audience.

"He asks the question that all of you want to ask but are afraid to. All of us eventually must face our own mortality. None of us knows how much earthly time we have. Let me answer the question this way. First, there is no need for Jesus to save you. You were saved on the day of the resurrection. Second, you will surely *not* die. You merely will take on a new form, as we all will. Consider the butterfly. It begins life inside of an egg and emerges as a caterpillar. After it is fully grown, the caterpillar builds itself a shell called as chrysalis, from the Greek word meaning "gold." Inside this golden cocoon, a wonderful metamorphosis takes place, and the caterpillar changes into a butterfly, breaking through the cocoon as a new creation to fly upward through the sky. You began as a small spark of life, an egg no larger than a grain of sand. You became a cell which grew and divided itself many times until you began to form into a shape inside of a sack in your mother's womb. A cord linking you and your mother provided food, water, and oxygen. You lived in an aquatic environment. You were quite a different creature than you are now. A human being, but not yet in the outer world. Slowly you grew within your nest. It was warm and you felt protected. It was all that you knew. But an irresistible instinct called you to emerge from the known to the unknown, and you entered this world still attached to a cord. You were cold, naked, screaming, and entirely helpless. You could not sit up, move from one place to another, feed yourself, or talk. Your form, the inner and outer essence of you, has been continuously changing ever since then. Some of the changes were slow, while others occurred very quickly.

"When you pass from the form that you are now, you will enter a stage much like the golden cocoon of the chrysalis of the caterpillar, but instead of calling it a cocoon, we call it passing over. Your physical body will be very much like the butterfly's cocoon. You will emerge from this stage in a form which our human senses cannot see or hear.

This new state of being is as real as the form you have now, but only God and the angels know this new form the soul takes after the cocoon stage. But the essence of you that began no larger than a grain of sand is indestructible and will not perish."

And so it went. The discussion lasted not an hour and a half but almost four hours. People stood in the audience and received simple answers to complicated questions. The monk's presence had slowly penetrated and spread throughout the audience. I had heard hundreds of lectures, talks, and speeches before, but this was quite different. He has . . . something, I thought to myself, but what is it? No new ground had been broken. True, he spoke from the heart and had never once used the word "I" all evening. True, he was a gifted speaker and the combination of his body language, his English in rich, Arabic brogue, and his appearance were a little unusual. But he really was doing little more than helping us remember what we already knew. Yet I felt good being in that audience in the presence of this man. I felt good like a little child feels good in anticipation of receiving a birthday present or going to the circus and riding on the merry-go-round. I needed to find out more.

After the discussion, I waited until the seemingly endless line of people who wanted to speak with the monk had diminished, then I walked over to where Father Nicholas was seated at the table in front of the room.

"Good evening, Father. I'm Larry Jetmore, and I wanted to tell you how much I enjoyed your lecture."

The old monk squinted up at me, turned his head sideways, and closely inspected me. After what seemed like a long time, he smiled, nodded, and said, "Thank you, my son."

He seemed to be waiting expectantly for me to continue.

"I was wondering if you might have some free time during the next couple of days. I'm a doctoral student attending a seminar here at the hotel, and I would really like to ask you some questions about your lecture."

The old monk and I ended up having breakfast together the next morning. His outlook on life and perception of the things happening around him were so different from mine. It wasn't that he took a Pollyanna-ish approach to life and denied the harsh realities of the world we live in; rather, he had an amazing ability to simplify what I thought were complicated moral and ethical subjects into a few sentences. He didn't waste his energy trying to convince anyone to adopt his views, he merely responded to questions asked of him.

The monk awakened in me a thirst for knowledge and an appreciation for the fact that when we are at peace with ourselves, that state produces an abundance of energy that can be transferred to others. I've had many more meetings with Father Nicholas, and we discussed the stressful nature of police work and the negative effects it has on police officers. This is the point of including the story of my encounter with Father Nicholas in this book on police ethics. Earlier, I mentioned how police officers are socialized to band together in a kind of secretive tribal society. I also touched on the fact that officers are continually exposed to the dark side of human nature and that this can lead to a "you're either with us or against us" esprit de corps and a need for psychological hardiness to do the work over time. I used the image of "living between worlds" to reflect the difficulty police officers have balancing what they are required to do in an "abnormal" work environment with what most people consider to be a "normal" world of family, friends, and the mundane events of everyday life.

Discussions with Father Nicholas helped me think through why so many police officers and other care-givers become disillusioned with leading lives devoted to serving others. When police officers are continually exposed to the worst in human nature, it is natural to become defensive, distrusting, distant, and callous. In addition, the fact that care-givers experience an almost physical pain when they realize that the enormity of people's problems are beyond their capability to solve results in an inability to balance one's life. We need to recognize that continual exposure to these types of experiences will affect us both mentally and physically, and we need to balance our lives by taking positive steps to improve the quality by engaging in activities removed from law enforcement. Police officers have a natural tendency to limit their contacts to people within their own tribe because they think that only other cops can understand the unusual world in which they work. As a former cop, I know that to some extent this is true. However, I

 Melchizedek was a mighty warrior

have also come to realize that over a long period of time this can result in a narrow, unhealthy view of life. Broaden your horizons. Explore other avenues of thought. You may find that you're a better police officer when you expand your contacts and add diversity to your life experiences.

☯ THE PHYSICAL SIDE OF A WARRIOR

How many police officers do you know with more than five years on the job who are physically fit or even healthy? Why is it that heart disease takes so many of our *warriors* at such a young age? How many officers in your department who are of retirement age are strong, vibrant, and ready to pull the pin with full confidence in their health and vitality?

Sad, isn't it? Policing is often a hurry-up-and-wait type of job. Long periods of inactivity are followed by sudden bursts of intense energy. Consider the following scenario.

It's the midnight shift. You're several hours into driving around on "aggressive patrol," which translates into several cups of coffee, a half pack or more of cigarettes, some routine motor vehicle stops, and getting your cruiser repaired by the night crew at the yard. Then suddenly, you spot a car whose occupants are wanted for robbing a convenience store. A high-speed chase ensues. Your adrenaline kicks in. It's the old flight or fight syndrome. Your body begins squeezing everywhere. Your eyes squeeze into slits so you'll have better vision. Your hands squeeze into claws so they can grip the steering wheel tighter. Your face squeezes up into a thing so horrible you'd scare yourself if you looked in the mirror. Your chest squeezes. Even your anus squeezes tighter so you won't have an accident while you're squeezing everything else. The wanted vehicle smashes into a parked car, its four occupants bail out, and now you're on a foot chase through back alleys and over fences. Your heart is pounding. You can barely talk into the radio. One of the kids you're chasing turns. There's something in his hand! You point your gun at him, ordering him to drop it. He does. You close the distance, get him spread eagled, holster your weapon, and prepare to handcuff him. He begins struggling violently. He's big and very strong.

Are you prepared? I don't mean just physically fit, I mean do you know how to defend yourself and those who depend on you, like the *warrior* you were meant to be? Do you know how to use your baton, blackjack, handcuffs, chemical deterrent, service weapon, and so forth? When was the last time you practiced with any of these weapons? Are you a student of the martial arts—karate, kendo, kung-fu, judo, hapkido, tae-kwon-do? Are you well versed in your state statutes relative to the use of force?

It's time to get yourself back in shape and then discipline yourself to remain physically fit as a lifelong commitment. All *warriors* are in tune with the physical side of their nature. You already know how to be in tune. Eat the right foods. Take your vitamins. Get enough sleep. Begin an exercise program. Start slowly, perhaps by walking. Then gradually combine some form of cardiovascular conditioning with a resistance exercise, such as weight lifting. Once you get yourself into shape, pick one of the martial arts that appeals to you, find a good *sensei,* and learn how to defend yourself and others. After studying white lotus kung-fu, tae-kwon-do, and hapkido, I found hapkido to be best for policing because it stresses hand-to-hand combat and the kinds of arm locks and come-along holds most useful in policing.

Continually conditioning the body is not an easy thing to do. It's easy to invent all kinds of excuses for not doing it. However, if you want to walk the path of a *warrior,* you must discipline the body and protect it with armor and shields that dragons and traps can't easily penetrate.

The greater the difficulty, the greater the glory.

Cicero

☯ THE MIND OF A WARRIOR

All things that strengthen the body and nourish the inner spirit are generated by the energy created in the mind. There is no harvest without the seed. In direct relation to what police officers see and do, and because they live between worlds, mighty armor is required to protect the mind from negative, self-defeating thoughts and behavior. The constant stimuli that our society bombards us with make it difficult to sustain the harmony necessary for generating the energy that allows the light to be shared with others. It's not hard work that drains our enthusiasm and zest for life; rather, it's how we deal with the emotional trauma surrounding and affecting us. Guarding the mind requires a combination of education, meditation, silence, and the persistent practice of positive thinking.

Most of a police officer's time is spent delivering social service to others—taking care of people. It has long been said in policing that an officer is part social worker, priest, doctor, lawyer, psychologist, and magician. To become a *warrior,* you must be more than just formally educated and street savvy. You must acquire wisdom. Wisdom is common sense with a twist. It's being able to reduce the complicated into simple terms. To know is more than to reason and intellectualize; it's also to grow in heart and spirit.

Because of the very nature of policing, there is continuous wear and tear on the body, mind, and spirit. The mind responds to trauma by establishing a protective barrier, resulting in a tendency to think only in terms of black and white. It's easier to function that way. It makes things less complicated for your conscience. However, such a lack of diversity in thinking produces a kind of numbness that limits personal growth and achievement. It creates a dull, black-and-white world where one day blends into another. That's why many middle-aged police officers look inside themselves and discover that nothing is there but the silence of lost opportunities!

When a man's fight begins within himself, he is worth something.

Robert Browning

It's time to take control of your life by disciplining your mind. Start by defining short-, intermediate-, and long-term goals. What is it that you want to accomplish personally and professionally? What would it really take to change? Is it time to go to college or to return to college for an advanced degree? Taking police-related seminars and training courses is good, but to grow and achieve your potential, you need the diversity offered by a college education. I know you work a shift plus extra hours to care for your family. I know that college costs money. I know it's probably been awhile since you graduated from high school or received your first college degree. Those are all excuses and rationalizations. Go to college! It's not just about getting a piece of paper so you can progress in the department. It's about gaining an appreciation for life and becoming energized by being around people who think and feel things differently than you do. It's only through diversity that change and growth occur. Nothing good comes easy!

Why not become a graduate student in your own profession? Self-learning was around long before our colleges and universities. What part of police work are you most interested in? accident investigation? forensics? bomb demolition? homicide? firearms? Choose a specialty, read all you can about it, attend schools and seminars, and become a nationally known expert. Commit yourself totally to new learning, and people will begin coming to you for advice and counsel, asking you to share your light with them.

Learn the art of self-reflection and analysis. Examine the following skills, habits, and abilities about yourself and strive to improve them:

The manner in which you speak and listen to others

Is your grammar and vocabulary appropriate for your audience?

Do you use good taste, manners, and courtesy when speaking with others?

Do you use a cheerful, warm tone of voice?

Do you respect the opinions of others even though they may conflict with your own?

Are you a good listener, or do you frequently interrupt others when they are talking?

Is it possible for you to disagree without being disagreeable?

The way you act physically

Are you physically graceful and poised?

Do you walk with confidence and good carriage?

How do you look?

How is your posture, physical fitness, and grooming and how
do they affect how you relate with others?

Your emotional harmony

Do you hide your emotions or display them in an appropriate way?
Are you emotionally balanced or do you project a dull or
negative outlook to others?
Do you analyze and reason through problems and
opportunities properly?
Do you jump to conclusions or reason from the facts?
Do you allow prejudice, tradition, and wishful thinking to
influence you?
To what extent do you use your abilities to acquire
knowledge?
Do you value time and use it to your best advantage?

Your ethics

Do you abide by the code of honor you swore to when you
pinned on the badge and became a police officer?

Are you ethical, moral, and trustworthy?

Your care-giving

How willing are you to help others?

How much of yourself are you willing to give without
receiving anything in return?

☯ SOME FINAL THOUGHTS

All of us have mentors. I was very fortunate during my police
career to have several "guardians" who pointed me to the "path to the
way." I wrote this poem in honor of one of the warrior-guardians who
appeared early in my career: Sergeant Foley. I was inspired to write it
after visiting him in a nursing home a few weeks before he went to the
great station house in the sky.

An Ode to Sergeant Foley

In a far-off place, in a different age in long ago time,
he was young to the badge and the gun.
Now the badge rests among torn and faded clippings
in a worn shoe box beneath the sagging cot where they
put the old warrior at night. None are left who know
from where he came or the battles he had won.
The vale of years has time collapsed. The dust of a Titan's
heroic deeds has sifted through the hourglass like a specter
flickering among twilight's shadowy sun.
Who will pay homage to the tall man in blue,
the peacekeeper who took the blood oath in the pale,
half-light of the red summer's moon? Warriors pure of heart
and living between worlds must pass beneath the shadow of
the cross before their earthly quest is done.

He is an old man now. He is just an old man now.
He sits in a wooden chair by the side window in a dark and
musty parlor amid other ancient sentinels. He does not look
out. The warrior drum still calls to him, but he has lost the
strength to go.
His withered right arm, once strongly muscled, lays useless
at his side. The great frame shrinks inward, twisted and
bent. Chest sinks, fingers withdraw to talons, the nose is
but a beak jutting from a skin-tight, sinewy face.
This is not the house where his table rang with the sound of
children's merry laughter. This is not the house where the lilt
of her voice lifted his weary brow. They will come to him
no more.
What's to become of Sergeant Foley, once minder of the lambs
at play? All who loved him long have perished, none are left to
shield his way. Who will find the worn old shoe box and wear the
badge he's tucked away?
Angels' wings softly flutter, sons of thunder clear the way.
Bagpipes peal their ancient banter, standard bearers light
the way. "Gallant warrior, why do you slumber? Your wife
awaits, your children play. Gallant warrior arise and greet
us, your time has come this very day."

References

Bly, Robert. 1992. *Iron John.* New York: Vintage Books.

Braswell, Michael, and Larry Miller. 1992. "Police Perception of Ethical Decision Making: The Ideal vs. the Real." *American Journal of Police* 11: 27–45.

Campbell, Joseph. 1990. *Transformations of Myth Through Time.* New York: Harper and Row.

Copenhauver, Martin B. "The Only Thing to Do." *Christian Century.* 19 October, 1994.

Day, Frank D., Robert Gallati, and A.C. German. 1974. *Introduction to Law Enforcement and Criminal Justice.* Springfield, Illinois: Charles C. Thomas Publisher.

Diehl-Dupont, Lis. "Officers Punished for Drinking Confiscated Keg." *Journal Inquirer.* 23 September, 1996.

Fletcher, Joseph. 1966. *Situation Ethics: The New Morality.* Philadelphia: Westminster Press.

Goldstein, Herman. 1975. *Police Corruption: A Perspective on its Nature and Control.* Washington, D.C.: Police Foundation.

Hitt, William. 1990. *Ethics and Leadership.* Columbus, Ohio: Batelle Press.

Horvath, Frank. 1993. "Polygraph Screening for Candidates for Police Work in Large Police Agencies in the United States: A Survey of Practices, Policies, and Evaluative Comments." *American Journal of Police* 12: 67–86.

Janofsky, Michael. "Philadelphia Agrees to Beef Up Supervision of Police." *New York Times.* 5 September, 1996.

Jewell, Anthony. "Indianapolis Police Chief Quits Amid Probes Into Officers' Drunken Brawl." *Associated Press,* 13 September, 1996.

Kant, Immanuel. 1963. *Lectures on Ethics.* New York: Harper & Row.

Kidder, Rushworth M. 1996. *How Good People Make Tough Choices.* New York: Fireside Book.

Kennedy, David M., Mark H. Moore, and Malcolm K. Sparrow. 1990. *Beyond 911: A New Era For Policing.* New York: Basic Books.

Klein, Jody, and Douglas Smith. 1984. "Police Control of Interpersonal Disputes." *Social Problems* 31: 468–81.

Klockard, Clark. 1989. "The Dirty Harry Problem." *Annals of Criminal Justice* 452: 33–47.

Kreyche, Gerald, F. 1993. "The Demise of Moral Authority." *USA Today*, September 1993.

Neiderhoffer, Arthur. 1967. *Behind the Shield: The Police in Urban Society.* Garner City, New York: Doubleday.

Posner, Michael. "Police Group Says 300 U.S. Officers Committed Suicide in '94." *Boston Globe,* 31 December 1994.

Reith, Charles. 1948. *A Short History of the British Police.* New York: Oxford University Press.

Rousseau, Jean Jacques. 1947. *The Social Contract.* New York: Hafner Publishing Company.

Senna, Joseph and Larry Siegel. 1996. *Introduction to Criminal Justice.* 7th ed. New York: West Publishing Company.

U.S. Department of Justice. 1988. *Report to the Nation on Crime and Justice.* Washington D.C.: U.S. Department of Justice, Bureau of Justice Statistics.

Wilson, O.W. 1977. *Police Administration.* 4th ed. New York: McGraw Hill Book Company.

INDEX

O

P

Q

R